T0341939

presents

FRAGILE!

by Tena Štivičić

TIASHA	Catherine Cusack
MARKO	Joseph Garton
GAYLE	Georgiana James
ERIK	Edward Kingham
MILA	Rayisa Kondracki
MARTA	Stella Maris
MICHI	John Moraitis

Director	Michael Gieleta
Designer	James Macnamara
Lighting Designer	John Terry
Sound Designer	Christopher James
Musical Supervision	Russell Hepplewhite
Voice Work	William Trotter

Producer	Rebecca Miller
Casting Director	Jim Arnold
Marketing	Natalie Galluccio
PR	Burning Issues PR
Publicity Design	Ben Pacey
Stage Manager	Katharina Berg Skomedal
Assistant Director	Lucy Taylor
Assistant to the Designer	Jason Wiggin

**British premiere 4th September 2007,
Arcola Theatre, London**

arcola
theatre

Preface

'Life is about moments. It's a mistake to think you can stretch them into a constant.'

I met Tena long ago, when we both lived Over There, At Home. She lived in Croatia, I in Serbia. Very close and yet a long dark tunnel apart. Between our two countries, a war had just ended. Or so they claimed. We both wrote plays, each on our own side of the border, while somewhere in the space between her and me, people kept killing and getting killed. Somewhere around, not so far from where we lived, there was a market where one could buy a woman. Also a colour telly, stolen cars, fake Marlboro, all kinds of drugs, heavy weaponry, if you really want to know, but also a real live woman. Once she is bought, for a few hundred dollars, she is the buyer's property and the seller refuses any further responsibility for the sold goods.

And the world around us, where we lived, was loaded with stereotypes. A woman should be stupid, and if she isn't she'd better not be pretty, and if she is she'd better be a whore, and if she isn't she'd better not be sensible, and if she is she'd better be evil, and if she isn't she'd better be stupid. You understand?

Life and death happen at great speed Over There, in our former countries. And so many of us go into hiding and isolation until That is over and the real life finally begins. But when That comes to an end and the real life still somehow fails to appear, when you try to glue the moments together and stretch them into a constant and even then it snaps, people run.

People run from the evil committed in their names, from watching it, from taking part or not taking part, from allowing it, from the shame, from the complicity. They tried to escape in different ways, to different places. As they run, they run into each other, somewhere in the big wide world, always carrying with them their indestructable emotional baggage. The load that follows you around everywhere you go and inhabits the faraway cities, and Tena's writing, for instance. The ones that can't escape the violence, even if they move thousands of miles; the ones that get stabbed and all they want is to call home, call their mum and make it better, but there isn't enough credit on the phone; the ones that have nowhere to take shelter – they live in Tena's world, the same world that I grew up in, the same world I started to write in. Because when you try to run away from who you are and who people think you are, from the 'better stupid than good' rule, you can't easily get very far.

When you leave Back There and arrive Over Here, you find yourself confronted with yet more stereotypes. A young artist from Over There is expected to embody the exotic Eastern European idea, or as Mila says in *Fragile!*:

'All the time I felt like they keep expecting me to do something unpredictable and wild, preferably sexual. Like I was some kind of an exotic eastern specimen that's, you know, got a trauma but shags like an animal.'

The concept is not very different to that market, although the approach is more subtle. Tena has the capacity to resist that, she writes great drama that magnificently reconstructs the vanished lives and never falls into the trap of the anecdote. She creates a world of her own, where people are both good and bad, guilty and confused, the destroyed and the survived, and destroyers of their own and other people's emotions.

Her world I recognise as my own, not only as my background and origin, but also as something I still have to live through. We both left Back There, we live divided by another border again, a real tunnel this time.

Like the boys in the play who are refused an entry visa because they didn't serve in the army (which is only necessary precisely because of those that did serve in the army), I have trouble getting into London from Paris.

So, although we sometimes see each other Over Here At Mine, our life is in the words, the letters, the plays we write.

She knows my world better than I know it myself, she knows that city that is my real city:

'Will you take me to Belgrade one time. Be-o-grad. White city. Beautiful.'

Biljana Srbljanovic, August 2007

Cast and Creative Team

Jim Arnold (Casting Director) Theatre includes: *Hortensia and the Museum of Dreams* (Finborough); *The Country* (Belgrade); *Orestes* (Lion & Unicorn); *100* (Camberley). Film includes: *Six Ways to Kill Your Lover* (Questionable Films).

Catherine Cusack (*Tiasha*) Theatre includes: *Factory Girls* (Arcola); *Salt Meets Wound* (Theatre 503); *Uncle Vanya* (Wiltons Music Hall); *Mary Stuart* (National Theatre of Scotland); *Mushroom Pickers* (Southwark Playhouse); *Brontë* and *Mill on The Floss* (Shared Experience); *The Gigli Concert* (Finborough); *The Gentlemen from Olmedo* and *The Venetian Twins* (Watermill); *Blood Red Saffron Yellow* (Drum, Plymouth); *Our Lady of Sligo* (Out of Joint/RNT); *Measure for Measure* (English Touring Theatre); *The Cocktail Party* (Edinburgh Festival Fringe); *Prayers of Sherkin* (Old Vic); *Mrs. Warren's Profession* (Lyric, Hammersmith); *Phaedra's Love* (Gate); *The Glass Menagerie* (Bolton Octagon); *Moonlight* and *You Never Can Tell* (Gate, Dublin); *Brighton Rock* (West Yorkshire Playhouse); *Bold Girls* (Hampstead); *Poor Beast In The Rain* (Bush); *Germinal* (Paines Plough); *Les Liaisons Dangereuses* (Ambassadors). TV includes: *Jonathan Creek*, *Ballykissangel*, *Coronation Street*, *Doctor Who*, *The Bill*, *Cadfael*. Film includes: *Finding Neverland*, *Conspiracy of Silence*, *The Lonely Passion of Judith Hearne*.

Joseph Garton (*Marko*) Graduated from the Guildford School of Acting in 2005 where he won both the Best Acting Male and Best Acting Performance awards. Theatre includes: *A Perfect Ganesh* (Cherub Company); *Ticky Tock* (King's Head). Radio includes: *High Table, Lower Orders* (BBC Radio 4). Joseph has also recently appeared in several television adverts and music videos.

Michael Gieleta (Director) Trained at Warsaw, Milan and Oxford Universities. Artistic Director of the Cherub Company. Theatre includes: *A Perfect Ganesh* (Gielgud); *The Way of the World* (Rose Bruford); *Hortensia and the Museum of Dreams* (Finborough); *Anyone Can Whistle* (Bridewell); *Last Song of the Nightingale* and *Change of Heart* (New End); *Twelfth Night* (Haugesund Festiviteten, Norway); *Company* (Oxford Playhouse); *The Marys* (Southwark Playhouse and Yvonne Arnaud, Guildford); *Still Lives* (British Council tour); *The Seagull* and *Two for the Seesaw* (Old Fire Station, Oxford); *Scenes from an Execution, White Chateaux, Artist Descending a Staircase, Last Train from Berlin* and *Stretching Strindberg* (Minerva, Chichester). As assistant director: *The Tempest* (RSC); *Heartbreak House* and *Arcadia* (Chichester). Opera includes: *Cavalleria Rusticana/I Pagliacci, Lucia di Lammermoor* and four vignettes, *Madama Butterfly, Tosca, Don Pasquale* and *L'Elisir d'amore* (South African State Theatre). Other directing credits include: *Oberon, Il Trovatore* and *Ernani* (Opera Integra); *Samson and Delilah* (Vision Opera). As an assistant director: *Queen of Spades* (Royal Opera House, Covent Garden); *Katya Kabanova* and *Carmen* (Glyndebourne). Michael has worked with Franco Zeffirelli on *Absolutely! (perhaps)* at the Wyndham's, and collaborates regularly with RADA, the National Theatre Studio and the Royal College of Music.

Russell Hepplewhite (Musical Supervision) Trained at the Royal College of Music. He won the Cherub Company's Theatre Alive! Composition Prize, and has since composed music for their productions of *Akhmatova's Salted Herring* (Menier

Chocolate Factory) and *Hortensia and the Museum of Dreams* (Finborough). Other composing credits for theatre include: *The Canterbury Tales, Everything Must Go,* and *The Canterville Ghost* (Southwark Playhouse); *Macbeth* (Creation, Oxford); and *Winter's Tale* (Mayfield Music Festival). Russell was Assistant Musical Director on *Oh What a Lovely War!* and *My Favorite Year* (Guildhall School of Drama). He has run workshops for English Touring Opera, and played in workshops at the National Theatre Studio. He plays frequently for musicals in the West End.

Georgiana James (*Gayle*) Trained at LAMDA. Theatre includes: *Flight without End, 4.48 Psychosis, The Duchess of Malfi, Macbeth, The Misanthrope, Three Sisters* (LAMDA).

Edward Kingham (*Erik*) Trained at the Royal Scottish Academy of Music & Drama. Theatre includes: *Some Voices* (Live Theatre Company); *All That Trouble That We Had* (New Vic Theatre Co.); *Woyzeck* and *Medea* (The Chandler Company); *Treasure Island* (Lyric, Hammersmith); *Noises Off, On The Razzle* and *The Captain* (Atheneum Theatre Co.); *Three Short Breaths* (Croydon Warehouse). TV includes: *Heartbeat* (Yorkshire TV); *Extremely Dangerous* (Patagonia Films); *Touching Evil* (Carlton TV); *The Round Tower* (Festival Films).

Rayisa Kondracki (*Mila*) Trained at LAMDA. Theatre includes: *Our Town, Tricycle* (Baby Grand); *Flight Without End, 4.48 Psychosis, Mathilde* (LAMDA). TV and film includes: *Wire in the Blood* (ITV); *Bourne Ultimatum* (Universal Pictures).

James Macnamara (Designer) Graduated in Art and Design from Pretoria Technikon, South Africa. He worked as a Senior Designer at the State Theatre in Pretoria until the closure in 1996. Over the years James has designed sets, costumes and lighting for numerous productions in South Africa including adaptations of popular international musicals like *The Buddy Holly Story, Return to the Forbidden Planet* and *The Fantastics*. He received the Hanekom Bursary in 1992 for outstanding contribution to theatre and in the same year his design for *Romeo and Juliet* won a Vita Award for Best Design. *Return to the Forbidden Planet* was awarded a regional Vita Award in 1998. Recent productions include: *The American Popess*; the multimedia dance work *Julia* with Jeannette Ginslov; The South African Music Awards for the SABC; as well as *Lucia di Lammermoor, Cavalleria Rusticana* and *Pagliacci* directed by Michael Gieleta. James has been a guest lecturer for the Entertainment Technology course at the Twsane University, for the Open Window Art Academy, Boston House College, and for the South African School of Film, Television and Dramatic Art, and serves on the Advisory Panel of the Entertainment Technology Twsane University.

Stella Maris (*Marta*) Trained at the Escuela Nacional de Arte Dramatico, Buenos Aires and the Guildhall School of Music and Drama. Stella is a member of ICAF (International Committee for the Artist Freedom). Theatre includes: *Necessary Targets* (Variety Arts Theatre); *Theatre for the Identity* (Arcola); *Sarita* (RNT); *Falkland Sound* (Royal Court and Traverse, Edinburgh Festival Fringe); *My Song is Free* (Drill Hall and Monstrous Regiment Tour); *The Portage of A.H. to St Cristobal* (Mermaid); *Chile Lest We Forget* (Westminster Hall); and most recently, work with AZ Theatre, including *Just War Stories, Palestine Verbatim*, and *Shock and Awe*. She has also performed *Crossing Frontiers* at the Poetry Café with actress

Anna Carteret. TV includes: *The Virgin Queen, Auf Wiedersehen Pet, Family, Between the Lines, Bambino Mio, Eldorado, Under the Sun, Die Kinder,* and *Nelly's Version.* Film includes: *Imagining Argentina, Hilary and Jackie, Truly Madly Deeply, Success is the Best Revenge, Electric Dreams.*

John Moraitis *(Michi)* John is a native New Yorker, and trained at the Actor's Studio. Theatre includes: *Crocodile Seeking Refuge* (tour); *A View From The Bridge* (Theatre Clwyd); *True West* (Dukes); *Julius Caesar, Merchant Of Venice, An Enemy Of The People, One Flew Over The Cuckoo's Nest, The Rainmaker.* TV includes: *Murder In Paradise, NY-LON, First Degree* (BBC Wales); *Office Gossip, People Like Us, Law And Order, NYPD Blue, As The World Turns.* Film includes: *United 93, Where The Truth Lies, Number One, Longing. Number Two, Regret, Goodfellas.* Radio includes: *For Your Pleasure, Baldi, Corona, Little Women, Red Elvis* (BBC Radio 4).

Tena Štivičić (Writer) Born in Zagreb, Croatia. She graduated from the Department of Dramaturgy at the Academy of Drama Art in Zagreb, and then completed an MA in Writing for Performance at Goldsmiths College, University of London. She took part in Future Perfect, the Paines Plough Young Writers Programme and the Royal Court's 50th Anniversary season, and BBC Bursary for young writers. Her new play *Fireflies* was commissioned by the National Theatre Studio in London. Her plays *Can't Escape Sundays, Perceval, Psssst, Two of Us, Goldoni Terminus* and *Fragile!* have been produced in Croatia, Serbia, Slovenia, Bosnia, Germany, Switzerland, Slovakia, Greece, Italy and the UK. *Fragile!* was awarded the Special Jury Award at Marulovi Dani Festival, Croatia; Best Play at Dani Satire Festival, Zagreb, Croatia; Best Play at the Borstnikova Srezanja in Slovenia; and the Special Jury Award for Theatre Innovation at Male Scene Festival, Croatia. In 2007, she co-wrote the play *Pijana noć 1918* [*Drunken Night 1918*] with her father, Ivo Štivičić, for Ulysses Theatre, Zagreb. Tena's latest project, *Goldoni Terminus,* was shown in July 2007 at the Venice Biennale. She lives in London and writes in English and Croatian.

Lucy Taylor (Assistant Director) Theatre includes, as director: *The Dateless Wonder* (Watermans, UK tour); *The Country* (Belgrade); *Breaking News: A Decision* (Theatre 503); *Attempts on Her Life, Not Not Not Not Not Enough Oxygen* (King's Head); *Timeless* (Windsor Arts Centre). As assistant director: *Pra Inglês Ver (For English Eyes)* (Royal Court); *Head/Case* (Belgrade/Swan, RSC/Soho); *Sun is Shining, Sami* (King's Head).

John Terry (Lighting Designer) John's work as production manager and stage manager has included international tours of *Interference* (Wishbone); and *Titus Andronicus* (Kaos); several national tours; and the circus big-top at Glastonbury Festival. As lighting designer he has worked in venues across the UK including the New End Theatre, the Shaw Theatre, the Finborough, the Royal Exchange Studio, Manchester, Battersea Arts Centre, Southwark Playhouse and Lyric Hammersmith Studio. He also works professionally as a director.

William Trotter (Voice Work) Trained Central School of Speech and Drama, Bristol & Exeter Universities. Company voice work includes: for the Cherub Company, *Edward II* (BAC, The Place, National Tour); *Hortensia and the Museum of Dreams* (Finborough); *Merchant of Venice* (Lyric Studio); *The Trial* (Riverside); *The*

Master and Margarita (Menier Chocolate Factory); *Gone Too Far* (Royal Court); *No Way Out* (Cochrane, Riverside). Private clients include: leads at Regents Park, Apollo Victoria, and various broadcasters. Actors' Centre tutor: workshops Multicultural Shakespeare, Vocal Truth for Stage and Screen. Also work with Escape Artists, Graeae, Mind the Gap, and the Magic Circle. Teaching includes: Arts Educational, Central School of Speech and Drama, Drama Centre, East 15, LAMDA.

Production Credits

David Burns (for **Burning Issues PR**) *mobile:* 07789 754089

Ben Pacey (Publicity Design) *web:* www.benpacey.co.uk

The Arcola Theatre

Arcola Theatre was founded by Mehmet Ergen in September 2000 when he converted a textile factory on the borders of Stoke Newington and Dalston into one of London's largest and most adaptable fringe venues. In just six years it has become one of the country's most renowned fringe theatres with a distinct and powerful identity both within the local community and British theatre.

For the Arcola

Artistic Director	Mehmet Ergen
Executive Producer	Leyla Nazli
Executive Director	Ben Todd
General Manager	Michael Harris
Finance Manager	Nicole Rosner
Associate Director	Serdar Bilis
Front of House Manager	Lauretta Barrow/Gemma Greer
Technical Manager	Roger Walpole

arcola
theatre

The Cherub would like to express special thanks to:

Mr & Mrs T.W. P. Arnold and T.W. Printing Associates Ltd
HDH Wills 1965 Charitable Trust
Royal Victoria Hall Foundation

Golden Roll Supporters

Lucie Bowman   Noel Casey   Pam Goold   Hilary King   Leigh Large
Sissi Lichtenstein   Holly Peryer   Laura and Ed Weeks   Jeremy White

Other Supporters

Richard Cazenove   Oliver Ford Davies   Kasper Nazeri   Sara Taylor

About the Cherub

The Cherub has as its mission to nurture, develop and produce
non-British dramatic works in the UK. It has been a creative
and pioneering force in British theatre since it was created in
1978 by Andrew Visnevski and Simon Chandler.

Artistic Director	Michael Gieleta
Producer	Rebecca Miller
Marketing Director	Natalie Gallucio
Literary Associate	Miriam Heard
Casting Associate	Jim Arnold

Board of Trustees

Noel Casey Nick Frankfort Michael Gieleta Pam Goold
Rebecca Miller Christopher Morahan Andrew Visnevski Phill Ward

Cherub Company London
9 Park Hill
London W5 2JS
Tel. 020 8723 4358
Fax. 020 8248 0318
info@cherub.org.uk
www.cherub.org.uk

FRAGILE!

Tena Štivičić

Thanks to Serge, Nino and Siv
for their stories

Characters

TIASHA, *mid-twenties, Eastern European*

ERIK, *mid-thirties, Norwegian*

MARKO, *late twenties, Serbian*

MILA, *late twenties, Croatian*

GAYLE, *late twenties, New Zealander*

MICHI, *fifty, Bulgarian*

MARTA, *fifty, Eastern European*

The play takes place in present-day London.

This text went to press before the end of rehearsals and may differ slightly from the play as performed.

Scene One

A barstool centre stage. A spotlight lights on MILA, *a pretty young woman in her late twenties. She is wearing a tight masculine striped shirt, a necktie and a pair of black trousers.*

MARKO, *a man about the same age, enters quietly.* MILA *doesn't notice him.*

MILA. Good evening. It's such a thrill to see so many of you here tonight. I've been away a long time and I must say I was a little nervous back in the dressing room. I thought, what if I go out there and the hall is empty. My ex-flatmates and some of those people that won the tickets when they bought an extra packet of tampons.

MARKO laughs quietly. She doesn't notice him.

I'd like to dedicate this first song tonight to all my student years of dreaming and dreaming in this city.

MILA sings. It's a slow bluesy song. She notices MARKO *and stops singing.*

I thought I was alone.

MARKO. You are good.

MILA. Yeah, well . . .

She's embarrassed. Therefore defensive.

MARKO. And you're funny.

MILA. You think? Oh, good.

MARKO. No, I mean it was funny. The joke about tickets.

MILA. Yeah, tampon jokes, I don't know . . . We are not open yet.

MARKO. I know. I wanted to speak to your boss.

MILA. Michi? You a friend of his?

MARKO. Not really. I'm looking for a job.

MILA. Oh. Well, we can always use a bouncer.

3

MARKO. I was hoping for something less . . . rough.

MILA. Yeah, well, weren't we all. No, I'm joking, it's not that rough. It's just sometimes, usually the Serbs, get drunk and emotional and, well, what's a better way to show emotions than pick a fight or smash a mirror.

MARKO. I'm a Serb.

Beat.

MILA. *Super, ja sam iz Hrvatske.* [Great. I'm from Croatia.]

MARKO (*cheerfully*). *Sestro!* [Sister!]

MILA (*coldly*). Easy.

MARKO. *Ja sam Marko.* [I'm Marko.]

MILA. Mila.

MARKO. Are you? [a play on words – *Mila* means 'dear' or 'kind']

MILA. Cute.

MARKO. *Otkad si tu?* [How long have you been here?]

MILA. Look, I prefer English.

MARKO. *Zašto?* [Why?]

MILA. Because: a) you need to practise, you don't want your accent to precede you.

MARKO. What?

MILA. Precede. *Bolje ti je da odma ne skuže po naglasku.* [Don't want them to see through your accent right away.]

MARKO. Aha. Okay.

MILA. b) you don't wanna get stuck with your community. There's no moving forward there.

MARKO. Right. Is that why you work in this place?

MILA. That's temporary.

MICHI *walks in. He turns the lights on. They reveal a bar to the left. This place is not a complete dump but it is one of those underground clubs that can never be properly aired and hosts people from countries where non-smokers are not to be trusted.*

MICHI *is a stubby, rough-looking man. He is essentially rude and uncultured, but has adopted certain manners of the rich western world that he can apply if he sees fit. He is the kind of man that leaves the impression of never listening to what other people are saying, but in fact has the memory of an elephant.*

MICHI. What is that? We open in half one hour. Go dress yourself.

MILA. I'm dressed.

MICHI. What, this?

MILA. Yeah, something wrong?

MICHI. No, it's beautiful. For a funeral.

MILA. Oh, please –

MICHI. How many times do I tell you – a little breast, a little thigh.

MILA. I'm not a chicken.

MICHI. You're not funny either.

MILA. Less is more, even you should know that.

MICHI. Yes, less dress, more skin.

MILA. I'm not trying to turn this into a concert hall. But a touch of, you know, class –

MICHI. Mila, you are performer. Like . . . plumber. Or . . . bricklayer. I am architect. You are bricklayer.

MILA. You should count your blessings to have a proper singer here.

MICHI. I light a candle every Sunday – thank you Lord for Mila. My clients is complaining. Too serious for them. People come here, they want to have fun. Fun is what makes money. If you want them cry, play their music so they cry for their mother, bottle of vodka, for their childhood, bottle of finest Merlot . . . You know our people. Eastern European soul, always bloody bleeding. You play that Brazilian shit, and jazz and soul, and my God, musicals – no bottles, no clients, no Michi's!

MARKO. It sounds great to me.

MICHI *had noticed* MARKO *but thought him less significant than the matter of* MILA*'s wardrobe. Now he turns to* MARKO *with a 'Now I'll deal with you' expression.*

MICHI. Yes. And you are?

MARKO. Hi. I'm . . . My name is Marko. I'm looking for a job.

MICHI. Yes? What can you do?

MARKO. I'm a comedian. A stand-up comedian.

MILA. Well, you've come to the right place.

She exits. MICHI *sits at a bar stool, his legs wide, he takes out a Davidoff cigarette and lights it. A heavy exhale.*

MICHI. Such cheek. Drive me crazy. (*Beat.*) Everybody is comedian here.

MARKO. But I'm good.

MICHI. Comedian, I have no use. Look at her, burst you laughing. No, thank you, bye bye.

MARKO. I'll do whatever. I can mix drinks. I can . . . Whatever you want. I'm not from here, I'm new –

MICHI. I would never guess.

MARKO. Vurzela said to contact you when I come to London. He said you will have a job for me. Or you will have someone who will have a job for me.

MICHI (*suddenly intrigued*). How do you know Vurzela? You are not Bulgarian.

MARKO. I'm Serbian. He used to be my father's supplier back in the –

MICHI. Ah, the good old days.

MARKO. – Communism.

MICHI. All days are good for people with positive thinking.

MARKO (*unconvinced*). Yes.

MICHI. Your father is big shot?

MARKO. My father is . . . He was a politician.

MICHI. But he was client of Vurzela. What, drugs?

MARKO. Oh, no. No drugs. Furs, leather. Jack Daniels, cigars, everything.

MICHI. Everything you need for decent living, yes?

MARKO. Yes, I suppose.

MICHI. And now?

MARKO. Oh, uh . . . he's retired.

MICHI. And Vurzela is businessman. How the wheel turns, no?

MARKO. Yes.

MICHI. And you – run away? Get yourself in trouble? Protest against government?

MARKO. No. I mean, yes, but that I . . . I just want a new start.

MICHI. Okay, Michi don't wanna know. In Michi's – discretion is important. Vurzela wants Michi to find you a job, Michi will find you a job. You say you can mix drink? You have experience?

MARKO. I worked in a cocktail bar.

MICHI. A cocktail bar in Serbia. What is world coming to?

MARKO. I know a few things about wine and brandy. And beer, of course. I see you serve Czech beer.

MICHI. We offer wide range of nostalgia.

MARKO. Think about expanding? Maybe a shooting range?

MICHI (*smiles*). Smart-ass. Let's see you make a Bloody Mary.

MARKO. Now?

MICHI. The floor is yours.

MARKO *goes behind the bar and starts making a drink.*
MILA *comes back in wearing a slightly more revealing dress.*

It's not a shit, but a dog's poo.

MILA (*annoyed*). Look –

MICHI. You think when you get into your precious musical you won't have to show skin.

MILA. That is different.

MICHI. What do you say, Marko, if you were a customer here and you were sitting down, having lovely drink, maybe little lonely, what you want to look at?

MARKO. I say, I want to look at a pretty woman. When she sings, even if it's 'London Bridge is Falling Down', I want to feel like she is singing it just for me. I want to feel like she doesn't notice there is anyone else in this room. Only me.

MILA *looks at him, ready to protest.*

MICHI. You don't want to see a little breast, a little thigh?

MARKO. If she's a good cook as well, I'll consider I am very lucky.

MILA *smiles.* MARKO *hands* MICHI *a Bloody Mary.*

MICHI. You two . . . I've been in this business long enough. You two are both fancy-schmancy. Tell me, Marko, how many steps you had to come down in here?

MARKO (*puzzled*). How many steps? I don't know, maybe fifteen?

MICHI. Twenty-two. Twenty-two steps down. Let me tell you, there is no fancy-schmancy twenty steps below the ground level.

MILA *and* MARKO *look at each other considering this piece of wisdom.*

But because I am having a very good Bloody Mary which always brings sun to my sky, I will give you no breast, little thigh tonight.

MILA *rolls her eyes, but knows that discussion is over. She pulls her dress up a little, letting the cut reveal a little more of her leg.*

(*To* MARKO.) And you . . . smart-ass . . . I will have to ring Vurzela.

MARKO. No problem.

MICHI (*exiting*). Hm . . . shooting range . . . Cynical is for staying home, not starting new.

MILA *and* MARKO *look at each other. They smile.*

Scene Two

A refugee hostel in London. A shabby office room.

TIASHA *is sitting in the office, waiting. She is a pretty, but jaded young woman dressed in simple clothes. She is looking around in discomfort, then leans over to inspect papers on the table, stopping to listen if somebody's coming. She goes over to a cabinet and looks at pictures and postcards displayed above it. The door abruptly opens and a small, elderly, chubby woman,* MARTA, *comes in.* TIASHA *looks caught in the act.* MARTA *speaks in a strong rough accent that doesn't reveal her origin.* TIASHA*'s accent is closest to Russian but her English is surprisingly good.*

MARTA. Ah.

> TIASHA *looks at her with discomfort.*

New girl?

TIASHA. Yes.

MARTA. Turn. Let me look you.

> TIASHA *doesn't know what to make of this woman but in the meantime obeys.*

Pretty girl. Nice bum, not grow any more.

TIASHA. What?

MARTA. 'What?' Who brings you up, wolfs? You say – 'Sorry'.

TIASHA. They told me to come here at four o'clock. To see Gayle?

MARTA. Ah. Yes. Gayle. Pretty girl – no boyfriend, unhappy. Young weeman – no man – go crazy.

TIASHA (*doesn't understand*). Yes. Are you a psycholog?

MARTA. You want to talk, talk to Marta.

> GAYLE *walks in.* GAYLE *is in her late twenties, rather plain looking, her clothes are colourful and all about layers. She speaks with a New Zealand accent.*

> TIASHA *pulls further back, almost hides behind the cabinet.* GAYLE *is carrying an armful of items that she puts down on the table.*

GAYLE. Ah, Marta. There you are.

9

MARTA. You call?

GAYLE. Yes, I need to talk to you.

MARTA. I must work.

GAYLE. No. Later. Marta, you know what this is?

> GAYLE *points to the pile of items on the table. A wooden shoe-size box, filled with items, a pair of glasses, a tin can, a pencil sharpener, some crumpled paper, some cotton wool.*

MARTA. Yes.

GAYLE. What?

MARTA. Your box.

GAYLE. Yes. My box. And why is my box important to me?

MARTA. Ah, it is art, you say.

GAYLE. Well . . . yes. I mean, it's my work and I've asked you several times not to treat it as rubbish. So why is it that I find it in the rubbish bin again?

MARTA. It look like rubbish.

GAYLE (*trying to keep her cool*). That is not for you to decide, thank you. I have an exhibition in two months and it's really really important that . . . Please, when anything looks to you like it could belong to my boxes, leave it as it is. Now . . . I've been doing the inspection today.

MARTA. Yes?

GAYLE. Well, I've noticed that the level of hygiene around here is not quite what it's supposed to be.

MARTA. Ah, pipple no care. Dearty, fealty pipple. Special that black boy new.

GAYLE. I wish you wouldn't call him 'black boy'.

MARTA. But is true. Is she white boy? No. Is she yellow boy?

> *'Yellow' makes* GAYLE *cringe even more.*

GAYLE. 'Yellow' –

MARTA. She black boy. Black boy not washing. That is simple true. She very . . . (*She mimics rage with her face and hands.*) after talk with you. Tttt . . .

GAYLE. Yes, he was upset but –

MARTA. You want I talk to him?

GAYLE (*frustrated*). No, thank you. You have to stop doing that. Please! It's my job to talk and yours is to clean. Which you haven't been doing, have you?

MARTA. I clean every day.

TIASHA stands there, behind the cabinet, behind GAYLE*'s back. Not really trying to hide any longer, but also not trying to find an opportune moment to make her presence known. Simply standing there, waiting to be noticed.*

GAYLE. I happened to be passing by the bathroom number three while you were cleaning and I noticed you only do the cleaning halfway up?

MARTA. You spying me?

GAYLE. Spying? I am your boss! I took the effort of going around all the bathrooms, both common rooms and kitchens, and it's the same everywhere, everything is cleaned halfway up.

MARTA *stands up energetically.*

What – where are you going?

MARTA. You look. Me, not big lady. Me – little lady.

GAYLE. Yes, but –

MARTA. Ploos, not so young. You know what deafficult is clean high. Arms hurt, shoulders hurt, cramps, terrible.

GAYLE. I realise, but we do have a ladder, why don't you use it?

MARTA. No! My head go dizzy on ladder. I fall, I break heap, then what? No work, no money, bye bye Marta.

GAYLE. Yes but, you're not doing the work. Don't you see? I wouldn't like to have to dismiss you . . .

MARTA. What – suck Marta? I speak with your boss.

GAYLE *notices* TIASHA *and stops talking.*

GAYLE. Oh!

They stare at each other.

Oh. (*She looks at the time, looks at her papers*.) Oh, of course. Ti . . . Tiasha?

TIASHA *nods*.

Oh. Well . . . Please, I'm sorry, I had no idea you had come in. Marta, did you know that Tiasha was in here?

MARTA *puts on a face of perfect naivety*.

Why didn't you tell me?

MARTA. Marta doesn't sticks her nose where it's not belong.

GAYLE. Right. Well, we shall have to speak later. In the meantime, please, consider this: if you do half the job, I think it's reasonable to pay you half the salary.

MARTA. What?

GAYLE (*showing her out*). I hope we've understood each other.

MARTA (*on her way out*). I no understand nothing. I only understand you want scam me. Every step rip off here, rip off there. (*She is now off.*) Bloody capitalism – thinks pipple is just kettle, look at this old weeman, she can't work, we take her to slaughterhouse, make sausages – what you watching, black boy? You take bath, you stink.

GAYLE *and* TIASHA *are both listening to* MARTA*'s voice coming in from the corridor.* GAYLE *takes a deep breath, then offers* TIASHA *a seat.*

GAYLE. What am I going to do with her? I'm sorry. What a welcome, ha? You speak English, don't you?

TIASHA. Yes.

GAYLE. Right, brilliant. That's Marta, she works here. She's a nice lady, although strong-minded. I'm Gayle.

TIASHA. Nice to meet you.

GAYLE. Have you settled in?

TIASHA. Yes.

GAYLE. Okay. Let's see. Basically, I am here to help you with practical stuff.

TIASHA. Yes.

GAYLE. You know what that means?

TIASHA (*pauses*). You are a psycholog?

GAYLE. Ah, no, not quite. Obviously I am here to talk if you want. And a psychologist can be arranged.

TIASHA. No, I don't need.

GAYLE. It's something to think about. It seems like you are dealing with your experiences in a very healthy way, but you know, traumas have a way of hiding and sneaking up on us when we least expect.

TIASHA. You had it?

GAYLE. What, a trauma? Well, we all have some, of one sort or the other.

TIASHA. What sort?

GAYLE. Oh, well, um, when I was five in New Zealand my mum slaughtered my pet lamb before my eyes. I think I'm fine, but every once in a while when I see anything like that I get nauseous.

TIASHA *stares at* GAYLE.

Not quite the same . . .

TIASHA. I had a dove. Birds are very important in my country. One time my father punish my brother for something we did together. My brother breaks my dove neck. And I always get, you know . . . (*Runs her hands over her body, tapping her fingers on the skin.*)

GAYLE. . . . Uh, goosebumps.

TIASHA. Yes, when somebody does this . . .

She puts her hands together, turns her palms out and suggests the sound of cracking links. GAYLE *repeats and actually produces the sound.* TIASHA *squeals.*

GAYLE. Oh, my God, I'm sorry! I'm sorry! Are you all right?

TIASHA. Yes. Yes.

GAYLE. I'm sorry.

A really awkward moment. GAYLE *despairs.*

Um . . . all right . . . So, we'll need to talk about . . . more recent events.

TIASHA. How I got here?

GAYLE. Exactly. Since we are applying for asylum, we'll need to go through everything from when you got taken from your country until now, in detail.

TIASHA (*lightly*). Okay.

GAYLE. You can do that?

TIASHA. Of course.

GAYLE *looks at* TIASHA, *unusually intrigued for a moment, but then goes back to the briskly business mode.*

GAYLE. Okay. That's good. In the meantime you'll stay here. We'll help you with anything we can . . .

TIASHA. I find work?

GAYLE. No. Unfortunately you will not be allowed to work while your case is being assessed. You will receive thirty pounds a week, (TIASHA *calculates in her head.*) and of course this accommodation. I know it's not very much . . . but people actually manage to do wonders with their rooms. Making them . . . personal.

TIASHA. How long it will take?

GAYLE. That's hard to say. Each case is individual. On average – two years.

TIASHA. Two years? Here? No!

GAYLE. I know it seems like a long time . . .

TIASHA. No! That is . . . No.

GAYLE. Please, calm down. Look.

GAYLE *gets up and starts explaining a graph that is hanging on the wall behind her desk. She assumes a teaching tone.*

This graph charts the usual progress of our clients. You see . . . the initial shot of energy upon arrival. 'I can do everything. Whatever it takes, I'm on my way up!' Then there is a sudden drop. Lack of energy, pessimism, defeatism. Nothing to worry about. Perfectly natural and short term. Then there is a slow but steady uplift. It's longer, more real. Followed by another drop, once you are faced with practical difficulties. That can go on for a while but again, it's only another natural phase. The intensity may vary from person to person, but these are all . . . steps . . . on the way to creating a happy and stable environment.

TIASHA. Where are you?

GAYLE. I'm sorry?

TIASHA. On the graph? Where are you now?

GAYLE *is startled and unprepared for that question.*

GAYLE. I'm a . . . I suppose . . . Well, it's designed mostly based on a different . . . kind of immigrants, um . . .

TIASHA *looks at her intently.*

But, I suppose I would be . . .

She inspects the graph and finds there is no way out. Then she points to the last part of it, where the curve drops again.

. . . here.

TIASHA. How long you are here?

GAYLE. Four years. (*Beat.*) But, as I said, this is a very loose interpretation. I don't really fit the frame.

TIASHA. Why did you come?

GAYLE. I've come here to study and then I stayed.

TIASHA. And you are not going back?

GAYLE (*slightly uneasy*). No. Well . . . I hope not.

TIASHA. Why? Is it very bad?

GAYLE. In New Zealand? No. If you like the sheep and the rain. And the smell of wet sheep.

TIASHA *doesn't respond to* GAYLE*'s humour.*

No, it's . . . small. And it's incestuous.

Again, no response comes from TIASHA.

I mean, everybody knows what everybody else had for breakfast and . . . You know?

TIASHA *nods. She looks at the box.*

TIASHA. Is that . . . what you study?

GAYLE. Fine art, yes.

TIASHA. And this is . . . (*Motioning around the office*.) like . . . humanity work?

GAYLE. You mean 'humanitarian'. No. This is actually my work. I don't quite live off my art. Not yet anyway.

GAYLE *finishes each sentence as if it is the end of this particular conversation. But* TIASHA *keeps questioning.*

TIASHA. You are good? You are good artist?

GAYLE. People always said I had talent. But . . . I suppose it's not just about talent.

TIASHA. What is it about?

GAYLE. Oh . . . um . . . it's work and patience and thick skin. Ultimately who you know and what's 'in'.

TIASHA. Like anything. When white girls become popular, then Asian girls are not so popular. Not 'in' . . . But that not means they are free, that means they are less value, so they are treated badly. Then they need thick skin. And patience.

Pause. GAYLE *tries to come up with something to say.*

GAYLE. Yes, that's . . . that's very . . .

GAYLE *is suddenly on the verge of tears.*

TIASHA (*looking at the box*). I like it.

GAYLE (*snaps out of it*). Do you?

TIASHA. Yes. It looks like you want to look inside. You shouldn't, but you want to. And pick things up and see what is under.

GAYLE (*taken*). Yes. Yes, that's what it looks like.

TIASHA. Like persons.

GAYLE. Exactly. You know, my mother had this box, and every once in a while she used to put something in it, something she cherished. She never really looked at it, just stored it in the box. For years. And then, when she died, I was nineteen, I opened the box and I started picking things up. It's funny what you can tell about a person from the trinkets they keep. It was like, with every layer of things I was chronologically going back through layers of her character. And when I reached the very bottom it was like looking at a different person. Someone she was years ago. Someone I never even knew.

TIASHA. Did you find something nice on bottom?

GAYLE (*smiles fondly*). Yes, I think so.

Pause.

TIASHA. You think I can stay? I hear all kind of people stays.

GAYLE. I can't guarantee anything, but we'll do our best.

TIASHA. There is nowhere to go back.

GAYLE (*pauses*). . . . I know.

TIASHA. What if I have somebody to help me? To help me settle in. Maybe I live with.

GAYLE. 'Somebody', as in, a friend?

TIASHA. Yes, a friend.

GAYLE (*suspiciously*). I wasn't aware . . . (*Going through her papers*.) that you had a friend in London –

TIASHA. I would have to find him first. It was a long time since I saw him.

GAYLE. Tiasha, you know it's important that you don't rely on your former friends . . .

TIASHA. Why?

GAYLE. If you are looking to stay it is extremely important you don't associate with people from your previous life.

TIASHA (*realising what* GAYLE *means*). Oh! No. He's not like that. He is someone who helped me one time already. He is journalist.

GAYLE. Right. A journalist.

TIASHA. Yes. A good man.

GAYLE. And you think this person would be willing to . . .

TIASHA. He promised he will take care of me.

GAYLE. Right. I suppose we can look into that. What is his name?

Scene Three

A newsroom.

Behind the desk, a number of TV screens light up. Apart from a few showing a weather forecast and some animals, most of them are showing war reports. ERIK, *a handsome thirty-five-year-old Norwegian man is sitting at the editing desk in a big leather office chair. He is on the phone and is simultaneously messing with the keys on the editing table. All the screens change to a new report that has just come in. Shots of shooting, explosions, blood, a wounded man screaming into the camera, an interior of a demolished palace.*

ERIK. Yeah . . . right. That's a good shot. Look at those uniforms, really bring out the colour of their gut . . . Good work, Matt. (*He laughs.*) What, you miss me? I don't know. I'm not coming back just yet . . . Yeah, they offered, but I'm all right for the moment. Night shifts put insomnia to good use.

MILA has come in. She is wearing a long leather coat and extremely high stiletto shoes. She is standing in the doorway. She has assumed a seductive pose waiting for ERIK *to notice her. By the end of his phone conversation, he notices her and smiles.*

Matt, gotta go. Hey, don't get yourself killed, man . . . We've got a bet running that those two Reuters twats go before you . . . Take care . . . I'm off . . . Cheers.

He puts the phone down. She comes very close. All through the scene she is very seductive and their conversation is like a prelude to sex.

Hey, how did you get in?

MILA. There's a Croatian guy working at the reception desk. I worked my charms.

ERIK. You people get around, don't you?

MILA. True cosmopolitans.

They kiss.

ERIK. Hi.

MILA. Hi.

Kiss.

You alone?

ERIK. Yeah.

MILA. Poor baby. All of this on your back.

ERIK. Dreadful, isn't it? But I get to edit. The truth is in my hands. (*He smiles playfully and kisses her.*)

MILA. Where were you?

ERIK. You smell like honey –

MILA. Where were you last couple of days?

ERIK. I had things to do.

MILA. What things?

ERIK. Oh, you know . . . things.

MILA. No . . . tell me. What are those things that you wander off to do and you're nowhere to be found for days.

ERIK. Two days.

MILA. Two days doing what?

ERIK. Mila . . .

MILA. Where –

ERIK. No –

MILA. I want to know.

ERIK. It's nothing. I just need to be by myself sometimes.

MILA. I don't believe you.

ERIK. It's true.

MILA. Where do you go?

ERIK. It doesn't really matter. Wherever is silent.

MILA. Where did you go now?

ERIK completely changes his expression. He turns grim. Suddenly they're not teasing any more.

ERIK. Mila, lay off!

She backs off. With her whole body. She feels this uncomfortable change of tone. But she pretends it doesn't bother her.

MILA. Well . . . Did you think about me?

ERIK *glares into her eyes, still frowning. Then a flirty smile flies across his face again.*

ERIK. All the time.

MILA. Liar.

ERIK. I did. I thought about this little spot right here.

He kisses her neck.

And here.

He kisses her cleavage.

And then particularly this spot. Here.

He puts his hand between her legs.

Wow.

He giggles. He opens her coat. A proud smile on MILA*'s face as she reveals her nude body underneath the coat.*

And the alarm didn't go off downstairs?

MILA. I blamed it on the shoes.

A giggle. A kiss.

ERIK *takes a little metal dose from his pocket. He taps some cocaine on her cleavage and snorts it. She giggles. Then he makes a line for her and she snorts it.*

ERIK *then starts kissing* MILA *passionately.* MILA *responds, but over* ERIK*'s shoulder, the screens catch her eye. War reports, shots of carnage and mayhem are playing on mute. Her eyes focused on the screens, she lets him kiss her, but her mind is somewhere else.*

Will you ever tell me –

ERIK (*between kisses*). Tell you what?

MILA. What happened in Bosna?

ERIK. You know what happened in Bosnia.

MILA. I want to hear it from you.

ERIK (*pulling back, annoyed*). Why?

MILA. Because. (*Teasing.*) Because it turns me on.

ERIK *considers. He sighs, as if she's won.*

ERIK. Once upon a time –

MILA. Seriously.

ERIK. It was a hot summer night. Dust stuck to our skin. The air was heavy. The smell of burning whirled up my nostrils.

MILA. What was burning?

ERIK. Grass, trees, sky. Flesh.

Pause.

They put us up in that pilgrimage site.

MILA. Medjugorje?

ERIK *nods.*

ERIK. Where Our Lady first appeared sometime in the eighties. Left some notes to some blind people or something. Of course, by now, she's more up-to-date. So at this B&B you get a fax with a message from Our Lady every morning. As if it were a weather forecast.

MILA (*sarcastic*). Did she have anything to say to you?

ERIK. No, she gave up on me. I did purchase a nice lamp though. In the shape of Our Lady supporting the lamp shade with her long languid arms. Very attractive. And for under ten pounds.

MILA *grows slightly – but cautiously – impatient. She's not getting what she wants.*

MILA. Right. A bargain. And then what happened?

ERIK. I found a rope attached to my window and stretching out into the distance.

MILA. A rope?

ERIK. A rope. I tried to follow it from the ground and see what it was attached to on the other side. But I couldn't. It was high up and it would get lost in the treetops.

MILA. What was it?

ERIK. The only thing to do was walk on the rope to see where it went. So I did. I walked on the rope. And it was the most amazing walk of my life.

A touch of scepticism appears on MILA*'s face.*

The things you see up there. Like nothing you've ever imagined possible. The people you've never imagined existed. Horror, delight. Danger, exhilaration. And no going back. Even though the rope kept getting thinner. Something wouldn't let me turn back. And then . . . there was an explosion, the rope snapped, I fell and everything went to black.

Pause. MILA *has by now realised this extended metaphor will not give her the answer.*

When I woke up I was in Zagreb. A new man. Quite literally, a new man.

He kisses her.

MILA (*slightly sulky*). You should be a poet.

ERIK. Turned on?

MILA. I just want to understand you.

ERIK. Now, where is the fun in that?

MILA. Not everything is about fun.

ERIK. You know, my lovely, talking is generally overrated.

MILA. Is that so?

ERIK. Yes. Getting rid of excess clothing on the other hand –

He goes to take her coat off.

MILA. You better enjoy this while you can. Michi wants me to strip in the club. You might have to pay for the pleasure in the future.

ERIK. Michi's got a good nose.

MILA. He's offering good money.

ERIK. Will you do it?

MILA. Are you joking?

ERIK. Come on . . . Look at you . . .

MILA. I'm serious.

ERIK. You do that way too often. Just turn serious with no warning and no justification –

MILA (*cutting him off*). It's one thing to do this for your – our – pleasure. Quite another to do it for money for the pleasure of drunken customers of a seedy bar.

ERIK. Well, that's a matter of perspective.

MILA. It's a matter of drawing a line.

ERIK *looks at her. A look of superiority. So much so that he can't be bothered to further explain. He smiles.*

ERIK. Not many women can walk in naked, offering sex and end up turning it into a moral debate.

MILA *is on the verge of starting a row.* ERIK *strokes her gently.*

Don't you think you have a responsibility to share this beauty with the world?

The frown begins to thaw. She indicates the screens.

MILA. Don't you have the responsibility to share that piece of news with the world?

ERIK. Actually, the world will be a nicer place without that piece. For another few minutes.

He kisses her.

MILA *smiles. She gives in. She starts kissing him back. As they kiss, the lights fade. Only the monitors still gleam in the darkness.* MARTA *appears in the shot. She speaks incoherently, through tears into the camera. There is a long line of refugees behind her, walking silently, carrying plastic bags.*

Scene Four

MILA *and* MARKO*'s flat.*

As cosy as a furnished, rented flat in Deptford can get. ERIK *is slouched on a sofa. Music coming from a CD player.*

MILA *is lying on the floor in her coat, humming to the song and obviously enjoying the floor.*

MARKO *comes in annoyed. He has a bruise on his face.*

MARKO. *Jao, bre, stišajte muziku.* [Hey, turn the music down!] (*He goes to turn down the music.*) For fuck's sake, you are both wasted. Look at the state of you. Can't you keep it down?

ERIK. Sorry, grandpa.

MARKO. Where've you been, one of those clubs where your shoes stick to the floor?

ERIK. You always assume the worst of us.

MARKO. Well, actually you, but I see that she is adjusting rapidly.

ERIK. As is your English. Is it that I inspire you?

MILA. He practises. Every day. Hours.

MARKO. *Mila, diž' se.* [Mila, get up.]

ERIK. Do you?

MILA. He does. Because when he masters the language, everything else is 'a piece of pie'!

MILA *and* MARKO *smile, obviously a private joke.*

ERIK. That's great. Self-confidence is half the job.

MARKO *tries to pick her up from the floor but she makes no effort to help, instead letting him pull her a few feet. She notices a bruise on his face.*

MARKO. Okay, suit yourself.

MILA. Hey, what happened to your face?

ERIK. Been up to something naughty on your own?

MARKO. I bet in your world that means masturbating to an inflatable doll.

ERIK. No, that would be a very dull Tuesday night.

MARKO *lights a joint.* MILA *sits up.*

MILA. What happened?

MARKO. Not-so-dull Thursday night at the club.

MILA. This happened at Michi's?

MARKO. Yeah. That Russian guy, Roman, brought a couple of girls. Under-aged, I'm sure. They all got terribly drunk . . . At some point Roman started to suck their toes.

MILA. Oh.

MARKO. What is it with women here? Why do they wear sandals in the middle of winter? Don't they make boots in this country? Their feet were all frozen and veined and, how do you say – *smežuran*?

MILA. Shrivelled.

MARKO *shudders*.

But the bruise . . . ?

MARKO. You know how pushy they can be with familiarity. The Russian insisted I join them, wanted me to drink brandy out of the girl's collar bone . . .

ERIK *giggles*.

And I wouldn't and you know, there was a bit of shoving . . .

MILA (*worried*). But you're okay?

MARKO *nods*.

ERIK. I thought with your dad being a big-shot commie, you'd be used to that kind of lewd behaviour.

MARKO. What would you know about that?

ERIK. Well, you know, Eastern Europe, mafia and politics go hand in hand –

MARKO. What, five minutes in Bosnia and you're an expert on Eastern Europe?

MILA. All right! Man.

MARKO. Anyway, even Michi was upset. He said, this is no place for such primitivism.

MILA. Michi said that?

MARKO. Yes, he said we have to sit down and rethink our policy.

ERIK. Who is 'we'?

MILA. We is Marko and Michi. Marko has become a pet at Michi's you see.

MILA *slowly drops back to the floor.*

ERIK. Does Michi know something we don't?

MARKO. I'm not a pet. He just wants a team.

MILA. For what?

MARKO. To make Michi's a legend. A home away from home or something.

MILA. Right. Such an altruist, our Michi.

ERIK. I don't think it's a bad idea at all. You boys should listen to your good old Michi. Somebody else will beat you to it – selling the sense of home, I mean.

MARKO *observes* MILA, *irritated.*

MARKO. I wish she would pick herself up off the floor.

ERIK. I think she looks sexy.

MARKO. She looks pathetic.

ERIK. Marko, my man, you really ought to try taking that condom off your brain.

MARKO. Thank you. I'll just pop to the bathroom.

ERIK. I gotta go.

MILA. No, you can't leave now.

ERIK. It's six o'clock in the morning, you should go to bed.

MILA (*whining*). I have to go to work.

ERIK. Call in sick.

MILA. Ah, I can't.

ERIK *bends down to kiss* MILA. *He slips the little metal dose into her hand.*

ERIK. A jump-start. I'll miss you, gorgeous.

MILA. See you tomorrow?

ERIK. Sure. Marko, I hope to see you real soon. Maybe we could go toe-sucking around town.

MARKO. I'll be counting minutes.

ERIK *exits.*

MILA. You are rude.

MARKO. Does that man have a nerve you can hit at all?

MILA. Oh, yes.

MARKO. Actually, I don't want to know.

MARKO *tries to pick her up off the floor and move her to the sofa. As he does, he notices she is not wearing anything under her coat.*

Oh, for fuck – you're naked!

MILA (*teasing*). So I am.

MARKO *looks at* MILA *with indignation.*

Oh, give me a break. Like you wouldn't like a naked girl to walk into your office and –

MARKO. Office? You went like that to his newsroom?

MILA. Yes. Is there a problem?

MARKO. Yes. What are you doing?

MILA. Having fun. We had a great time.

MARKO. I bet he did. The question is – did you? Did you have a great time on the tube going there?

MILA. Marko, you don't get it. Not everyone is the same as you.

MARKO. No, but you are.

They are both silent. He drops the subject and in a more friendly voice:

How the audition go?

MILA. I tripped up.

MARKO. You'll wake up one day and see your feet through your nose.

MILA. That's funny. Ever tried working as a comedian?

MARKO. You should be practising and not waste time with that nut.

MILA. I tripped up. It happens. Nothing to do with . . . anything. It was a shit musical anyway. I don't want to be in shit musicals. I want to be in good musicals. With great music and with a story and with a fucking message I can relate to.

MARKO. Right. Which is what musicals are known for.

MILA (*like Humphrey Bogart in* Casablanca). Well – I was misinformed.

27

They laugh.

Seriously. You know, you probably don't cos you're a boy
and you're . . . cool but sometimes, there are these songs,
really great songs with a great orchestra and . . . Shit
musicals in shit theatres are not exactly what I dreamt of.
(*Pause.* MILA *gets up.*) I have to get dressed. Make me a
cup of coffee? Turkish? (*Exiting.*) You know, this would be
an altogether better country if they knew the smell of
Turkish coffee in the morning.

MARKO *stays on the sofa.*

MARKO. Why him?

MILA (*off*). Because I'd rather live in Hoxton than Deptford.

MARKO (*giving up*). Right.

MILA *comes back buttoning a nurse's uniform.*

(*Sarcastically.*) What, another show for Erik?

MILA. Very funny. (*Pausing to think.*) Shit, I never thought of
that.

MARKO *rolls his eyes. She smiles.*

So easy to get you worked up.

Silence.

Because he's Scandinavian, they're reliable.

MARKO. Is that what they are?

MILA. Yes, reliable and safe. Like those – remember the
Scandinavian UN soldiers. They never stepped on the grass
in parks. Never smoked in non-smoking areas.

MARKO. But then they beat up a prostitute.

MILA (*cornered*). Why do you try to make him into a villain?

MARKO. He is a fucked-up cokehead and you're making him
sound like a retirement fund.

MILA. It's a phase. He just needs to be saved . . . a little. How
'bout that coffee?

MARKO. You are putting your money on the wrong horse,
'gorgeous'. He isn't more typical for Scandinavian than you
are for Croatia. That's why we all leave, because we don't

fit in. How long do you think you could go round visiting your boyfriends naked before you get ostracised in Zagreb?

MILA. Exactly!

MARKO. And how long do you think he could do it in that little village in Norway?

MILA. I don't underst –

MARKO. And with the shit he went through, he could end up pulling your heart out in his sleep.

MILA. No, actually, that sounds more like your heritage.

Beat.

MARKO. I'm going to bed. (*Exiting.*) You know, the kind of person you pretend to be, you should have Michi wrapped around your little finger.

MILA (*to herself*). And you are typical.

MILA *gets up, looks at herself in the mirror; does a few dance moves.*

He would love this.

Scene Five

MICHI*'s bar.*

ERIK *and* GAYLE *are sitting at the table.* ERIK *is staring into his glass.* MARKO *is behind the counter, washing up.*

GAYLE (*uncomfortably*). It's a lovely place. A bit dark. But has character, I suppose. (*Pause.*) And there's live music in the evenings. I really should come and see one night. Is it . . . Eastern European . . . music?

ERIK (*sarcastically*). You mean, do they sing in the Eastern European language?

GAYLE. Okay, fair enough. Look. I realise, it's a shock. Which is why I thought it might be good that I made the initial approach.

ERIK. I thought you just wanted information. Like . . . to help with refugees.

GAYLE. Yes. Well, I couldn't very well tell you over the phone.

ERIK. I thought she was dead.

GAYLE. Yes. She's not.

ERIK. She is in London.

GAYLE. Yes. And I have a strong impression she's come here to look for you.

ERIK. But . . . I thought she was dead.

GAYLE. Yes, you've said so.

ERIK. They stuck a grenade into her mouth. (*Pause.*) Pushed her to the floor, poured beer on her, pulled her hair and shoved a hand grenade into her mouth.

GAYLE. Yes. From what I've managed to gather, that was not the grenade that actually exploded. There was another one that caused the explosion. Not that one. Which is how she survived. Which is how you survived.

ERIK. How do you know about that?

GAYLE. I've done my homework.

ERIK. Yeah, but – I – thought – she – died.

GAYLE. I – under – stand.

ERIK. Sorry.

MICHI (*as he enters, talking on the phone*). No, Roman, now is the time, friend. The map of Europe is about to change. We must saddle that horse. My friend, your face in Michi's always bring sun to my sky. I am looking forward.

He puts the phone down. He observes ERIK *and* GAYLE. *He looks at* MARKO *as if to ask 'What's going on there?'* MARKO *shrugs.* MICHI *sits at the bar, lights a cigar, motions for a drink, takes out his Blackberry and begins calculating. Occasionally he glances at* MARKO, *who is watching* GAYLE.

GAYLE. The owner, I assume?

ERIK. Yes. A sweetheart.

ERIK *feels trapped. And breathless.*

GAYLE. Look. I don't know how you've dealt with what happened to you. You seem fine, although your lifestyle would suggest that maybe you're compensating for something and –

ERIK. And what exactly do you know about my lifestyle?

GAYLE. You've got quite a reputation for . . .

ERIK. Yes?

GAYLE. Some would say 'living life to the full'.

ERIK. I see. And you would say . . .

GAYLE. I didn't come here to judge you. My concern is not with you.

ERIK. That is very thoughtful.

GAYLE. And because of that I've persuaded her not to surprise you and let me come and . . . ease the shock.

ERIK. Smart.

GAYLE. But, she is ready to see you. Tomorrow even.

ERIK *looks at* GAYLE*; there's a touch of panic there, but he does his best to conceal it.*

ERIK. You're not giving me much time.

GAYLE. She seems to think you'd be thrilled to learn about her.

ERIK *is silent, obviously thinking intently.*

ERIK. Of course I'm thrilled. She's alive. I feel like I'm suddenly in a soap, but I'm thrilled.

GAYLE (*shocked by his comment*). This is not a humorous situation, you have no idea –

ERIK. I know, I know, I know . . . Don't start freaking out. I'm just buying time, obviously. You work with people, you should know a few basic patterns.

GAYLE (*uncomfortably*). Yes. Well –

ERIK. It's like a ghost coming to visit.

GAYLE. She's no ghost. She's a young woman. And she hasn't come to visit.

ERIK. . . . Uh . . . is she . . . normal?

GAYLE. Normal . . . That's a very tricky word.

ERIK. I would think she'd want to go home.

GAYLE. Yes. I don't think her home is the happiest of places on this planet.

ERIK. But London is?

GAYLE. It's where you are.

ERIK. So, you're just gonna dump her on me?

GAYLE. I wasn't aware you would look at it that way.

ERIK. No, I mean, I thought she'd be in some sort of a system now, or something. It's really stuffy in here, isn't it? I wish (*He shouts out.*) you aired this place once in a while.

MICHI (*not looking at him*). Too much air is very bad. You can go crazy thinking.

GAYLE. There is a whole procedure for asylum seekers –

ERIK. Will she get it?

GAYLE. Oh, she'll get it. She's had more human rights violated than all the rest of my clients put together. But she's not allowed to work in the meantime, and in order to get affordable accommodation she ought to stay in the hostel. And that can be . . . depressing. It's kind of . . . no man's land.

> ERIK *is silent.* GAYLE *is uncomfortable. He's not a man with whom silence is a comfortable option.*

Um . . .

ERIK. I need a breath of fresh air. I'll be right back. Have another drink.

> ERIK *leaves.* GAYLE *is left wondering. She observes* MARKO *but then looks away and tries to appear at ease.* MICHI *points to a glass with his head and then points to* GAYLE. MICHI *tends to give orders using body language rather than words.* MARKO *smiles – he has already begun mixing a fresh drink. He goes over to* GAYLE's *table.*

MARKO. Another one?

GAYLE. I don't know really –

MARKO. On the scale of one to ten, I say eight – he comes back.

GAYLE. You think?

MARKO. Unless you're carrying his child. In that case, he'll be on the plane to Baghdad by now.

GAYLE. You know him well?

MARKO. Reasonably. (*Puts her drink on the table.*) He is dating my flatmate.

GAYLE (*astonished*). Oh.

MARKO. Hope I didn't spoil it.

GAYLE. Oh . . . no. No. I'm not . . . This is really a business meeting, nothing more.

MARKO. Oh, yes, we're a popular destination for 'business meetings'.

GAYLE *giggles.*

I'm Marko.

GAYLE. Gayle. Nice to meet you.

MARKO. Pleasure, Gayle, enjoy your drink.

GAYLE. Oh, I think, maybe, a Diet Coke –

MARKO. Miss Gayle. Off the top of your head, does this look like establishment that has Diet Coke?

She blushes.

On the house.

GAYLE. Thank you, that's very kind.

GAYLE *leans a little to catch* MICHI's *eye and thank him as well.* MARKO *stops her and whispers.*

MARKO. In East Europe, it's very rude to thank a man for buying a woman a drink. They think you're mocking them.

GAYLE *leans back, instinctively taking the advice and looking somewhat confused.*

I'm joking.

GAYLE (*relieved, smiling*). Oh . . . Oh, God. Either I'm appallingly gullible or you're really good.

MARKO. No – I'm good. You see, I'm not really a bartender. But hey, I'm not an actor!

GAYLE. Writer?

MARKO. Comedian.

GAYLE. Really? I think that's a noble profession.

MARKO looks at GAYLE suspiciously.

No, I do. I think it's one of the few professions that make sense. Making people laugh.

MARKO. Well, thank you. I think that exact thing.

They look at each other and smile. GAYLE is suddenly embarrassed and breaks the silence.

GAYLE. I'm not really a social worker. Not that you knew I was a social worker. But I'm not, really.

MARKO. I've got a theory about social workers.

GAYLE. Hm, do I want to hear it?

MARKO. Maybe on our second date.

GAYLE smiles. It's not very professional but she can't help being won over.

GAYLE. In fact, I wouldn't mind, I'm sure. I'm not particularly proud of it. Or good at it, I'm afraid.

MARKO. I'm sure you are. You have a kind face.

GAYLE smiles, embarrassed.

So, what are you then?

GAYLE (*with mock solemnity*). I'm a conceptual artist.

MARKO. Uh, I've got a theory about them as well.

GAYLE. I'm sure.

ERIK comes back in. Seeing MARKO with GAYLE, he suddenly realises where they are. MARKO, MICHI, MILA, really don't need to know about this. He looks at MARKO, suggesting that he leaves and gives them privacy. MARKO goes back to the bar.

ERIK. We should go somewhere else.

GAYLE *wouldn't exactly mind leaving, but she's alarmed by* ERIK's *erratic behavior.*

GAYLE. Why?

ERIK. It's stuffy in here.

GAYLE. It's pouring outside!

ERIK, *trapped, sits back down at the table.*

ERIK. Okay. I'll come to meet her tomorrow.

GAYLE. If you can't handle it, I can . . . understand that completely. I think she'd be broken, but I understand if you have a relationship and your career . . .

As she says 'relationship', she vaguely gestures in MARKO's *direction.*

ERIK. Not an idle second with you, huh?

GAYLE. Look, I just . . . I think the worst thing would be that you come back into her life and then decide to drop her. She's not strong enough for that.

ERIK. You're an artist, yeah?

GAYLE. You've done your homework as well.

ERIK. Yeah, I like to do detective work on people. Relaxes me during those long night shifts.

GAYLE (*bitterly*). Better that than child pornography.

ERIK. Or sleeping with victims of trafficking.

Pause. GAYLE *looks at him sternly.*

Sorry. That wasn't funny. (*Pause. Then, in a tone that's inappropriately threatening:*) Do you find inspiration in the people you work with? Do you feed on the tragedies? Do you think you possess awareness?

GAYLE. What?!

ERIK (*casually*). I'm sure they're not paying you to monitor my lifestyle.

GAYLE. No.

ERIK. Then why?

GAYLE. I want to help her.

ERIK. Why?

GAYLE. She's . . . worth it.

ERIK. She never liked pity.

GAYLE. It's not pity. It's admiration.

Pause.

ERIK. Four o'clock then?

GAYLE (*hesitates*). This is the address.

They get up to leave.

(*To* MARKO.) Bye. Thanks.

MARKO. Goodbye, Gayle. Drop by sometimes. Feel as free as a stranger. We all do.

GAYLE. Yes, um . . . Maybe.

ERIK *and* GAYLE *exit.* MICHI *observes* MARKO.

MICHI. Easy, boy.

MARKO. I'm just being a good host.

MICHI. You should better think about business than skirt.

MARKO. I am thinking about business. I've got two amateur festivals next week and notice how my English is progressing daily.

MICHI. Fooling around. I mean real business.

MARKO (*carefully*). What kind of business?

MICHI. Marko, my boy, the map of Europe –

MARKO. – is changing even as we speak. I know.

MICHI. . . . even as we speak. Excellent. You are better. I know from first day you will go far.

MARKO. Oh, yeah?

MICHI. Oh, yes. And this is moment to act.

MARKO. How?

MICHI. How? All this people will come to UK now, some to work, some to visit, some to try luck. All will think – easy, we are one now! But, haha, what a surprise, do you think England will say – welcome brothers, what can we do for you? Bollock!

MARKO (*faking naivety*). No . . . you think?

MICHI. This is where we come in. Expand business. Offer rooms, offer entertainment, offer 'comfort', food maybe. Compass, so to speak.

MARKO. With UK prices.

MICHI. Competitive. But not rip off!

MARKO. Risky.

MICHI. No risk no profit.

MARKO. And what do you want me for? Make beds? Grill *ćevape*?

MICHI. We will need starting capital.

MARKO. Should I rob a bank?

MICHI (*seriously*). You could get some capital. And then you could be full partner.

There is a moment when the two men look at each other intently like they have a secret.

MARKO. I don't know what you're talking about.

MICHI. Come on –

MARKO. No.

MICHI. You think that is mature. But it is stupid, it is juvenile. It would be mature to accept what can help to become independent.

Pause. They stare into each other's eyes.

MARKO. No.

MICHI (*retreating*). All right. Mimosa. You don't know this because you are young. But when time starts running out, there is moment when you have to decide. I am going to splash around safe in the shallow or I'm going to jump on the big wave. (*His phone rings.*) Think about it. (*Into the phone.*) Halo!

MICHI *exits.* MARKO *absentmindedly washes glasses.*

*

MILA *is on the other side of the stage, speaking into the phone. He is not picking it up.*

MILA. Erik, where are you? Hey, you know how I blew that audition for . . . Well, turns out assistant director is a director himself. Yes. Well, not high profile, obviously, but he rang me to say that he thinks I would be perfect for a part in a play he is directing in . . . Can't remember what the theatre's called. Isn't that great? A proper part. With singing. Call me, we have to celebrate.

Scene Six

The hostel.

TIASHA *is waiting. She is visibly nervous. She straightens the sheets on the bed. She fluffs up the pillow. She adjusts her hair, looks at herself in the mirror, picks her hair up then releases it.* ERIK *appears silently. He watches* TIASHA *in front of the mirror. She didn't notice him but there is a moment when she feels his presence. She turns around. They stand some way apart from each other. The silence is charged with years of unspoken words.*

TIASHA *cries out. She encloses her nose and mouth in her hands and produces a sound of excitement; it is an icebreaker of sorts.* ERIK *opens his arms, and gives her a charming, inviting shrug. She rushes to his embrace and gives into it completely. He is somewhat reserved but trying to hide it.*

Still, no words. Heavy breathing.

Finally . . .

ERIK. Hey.

TIASHA *breathes.*

Hey.

TIASHA *wants to speak but can't.*

Hey, cricket.

TIASHA. Hey.

ERIK. Let me look at you.

TIASHA *takes a step back.*

Silence.

TIASHA. Woman.

ERIK. Beautiful.

They look at each other. ERIK *looks down.*

TIASHA. What?

ERIK (*quickly looks back into her eyes*). What? Nothing.

TIASHA. I . . . think, thought, all the time I thought, what I
will say when I will see you. All the time. One time I
thought I will see you in the street and I thought I will say I
will ask for direction and you will then see it is me and be
surprised. Other time I thought I will see you on airport, and
many other times, I have hundred conversations in my head,
so many first thing I will say to you when I see you and now
I don't know and I don't remember even one of them.

She stops abruptly. She has to take some air.

ERIK. Your English is better.

TIASHA. It can be much better. I have learned it. (*Getting
angry.*) I don't know why is it so bad now. I learned. I got
tapes and walkman. Dado think, thought I am listening to
music.

ERIK. Dado? The bastard is still alive, ha?

TIASHA. Dado is in Sweden. He is running jewellery shop.

ERIK. What? (*With sudden rage.*) He should be doing a
million years in jail.

TIASHA. No one is in jail.

ERIK. How come he gave up slave-trading? Became too soft
for him?

TIASHA. Everybody gives up sometime. It's not so easy when
there isn't war going on.

She stops again. Looks at ERIK *and grins.* ERIK *smiles
back, but awkwardly.*

You are shocked.

ERIK. Tiasha . . . I dream about you sometimes.

TIASHA. You do?

ERIK. They are not good dreams.

TIASHA. Oh.

ERIK. I mean they're nightmares and . . . You know.

TIASHA. But I'm here now. Look, real, live. And it's not nightmare here.

ERIK. Well . . . Tiasha, we have to . . . I don't know what we have to do. Isn't that just what you need . . .

ERIK*'s phone rings.* TIASHA *notices. He doesn't pick up. When it stops ringing he switches it off.*

TIASHA. I know. You have a life. Gayle said. But I know that. That is all right. I can wait. I have no problem to wait. It is much easier to wait now because now I am here and I am free. I am happy. So I wait. Until you are ready.

ERIK. I tried to find out, when I got better. They said everybody died. No survivors. Not even any evidence of them ever being there. Convenient, isn't it? The place was bombed to the ground the next day.

TIASHA. You looked? For me?

ERIK. Yes.

TIASHA. Because . . . you said you would.

TIASHA *holds him as if to comfort him.*

ERIK. Gayle said they took you all over Europe.

TIASHA (*after a pause*). Dado took me to Kosovo. And he sold me there. He said I was bad luck. He said women are never safe investment. Then they took me to Italy. On a boat. In a bag. Italy was all right. Woman who had the brothel, had a sick husband. I wash him and massage him. Not much he can do. Sometimes he wants to watch me touch myself. He says he doesn't care what happens to her, bitch. He promised when he is dead, important people will get letters telling everything about me, and business and bitch. I will be saved then. He died and I wait. But nothing. He was a liar. I got so sick waiting, my hair falled off and I lost six kilograms. Bitch got angry and passed me to go on. (*Mapping her journey in her head.*) After that Finland. Finland was rough. Men drink lot. And they are violent. But violent in different way. More imagination.

ERIK. Wh . . . Never mind.

TIASHA (*amused*). Did you know there are places where men drink more than in Balkan?

ERIK gives a slight laugh. The story is nauseating to him, especially the strange humour TIASHA seems to find in some of it.

You remember there was UN guy from Finland in Bosna? You remember? He was always trouble.

ERIK. The one that used to cut and burn girls.

TIASHA. Yes! That one. I come to Finland, my second customer – knock knock – he is there.

ERIK stares.

World is village, no? But, he don't cut me or do anything very bad any more. Because, I am different. I'm not shivering and shaking and crying any more. I am strong. And also, I am very good.

ERIK. And by that you don't mean obedient.

TIASHA. It's funny. First I just lie there and wait to be over. Then I understand if I do effort it can be much more easy and much more quick. More easy to be a good prostitute than a bad prostitute.

ERIK. You weren't a prostitute.

TIASHA considers. Then she switches back to her story.

TIASHA. In Finland I am cold all the time. I would think – oh, my God, what if Erik wants to go back home to live? Norway is too cold for me!

She laughs again like she said, sometimes silly, like a little girl. ERIK smiles, but it is a sour smile. He touches her face.

ERIK. My dear, my dear, dear . . .

TIASHA. And then I saw you!

ERIK. You saw me?

TIASHA. On television! When you were reporting from South Africa. And I saw you were with news agency again. Oh, you look just the same. A little less hair, maybe, yes?

She giggles and strokes his face. He doesn't know how to react.

ERIK. Tiasha . . . How did you get here?

TIASHA. The last year, I knew ways. To get out. To run away. Because, sometimes they make mistakes. Very . . . How do you say opposite from 'often'?

ERIK. Seldom.

TIASHA. Sel-dom. They make mistakes seldom . . . seldomly?

ERIK (*impatiently*). No, just seldom. Go on.

TIASHA. Sometimes they are not careful. But I am so busy being scared that I don't notice. But, last year, I'm not much scared any more – then I can pay more attention. I find this nice man from Montenegro. He worked like . . . like . . . man kicking people out of a club?

ERIK. A bouncer.

TIASHA. Yes. And he got me fake passport. Then I wait. House where I was living and some other girls – one time a month they would have parties for their regular clients. Especially if there was new girl, virgin that was just brin . . . brought to Finland. Then they would have like a spectacle, like a show in the house. But I was always with this one same man, very nice, older, sweats a lot, very kind. But I had to hit him with his laptop. And I jumped out of the window. I twisted my ankle but I didn't feel it until I got on the plane. On the plane! Alone!

And then I am here.

Silence. TIASHA is waiting for ERIK to say something.

ERIK (*after a long pause*). It's been years.

TIASHA. Yes. Tell me about you.

ERIK. So much has happened.

TIASHA. Yes. Tell me.

ERIK. We are different.

TIASHA. I'm not. I'm the same I was last time. Well except I am little thinner. And I don't use drugs.

ERIK. Really? Did it get very bad?

TIASHA. Not very bad. But you can't trust your instinct when you use drugs. And I had to trust it. That was everything I had.

ERIK. I'm not the same.

TIASHA. You look same. (*Smiles.*) You talk less.

ERIK. Half of me is not me, Tiasha. They gave me a kidney of an eighteen-year-old boy who crashed his bike into a wall. He crashed his fifteen-year-old girlfriend along. Her head cracked open on the road in front of the Sheraton Zagreb Hotel. She was dead instantly. On the way to the hospital, he must have been thinking, I killed a girl. My girl. Someone's daughter. Fifteen year old. Old enough to have a baby, not old enough to drive. I carry his kidney around. The blood I got back in Bosna. Imagine where that blood's been.

TIASHA. Your mind and heart is still your, yes?

ERIK. Yes.

TIASHA. Then you are still the one I know.

ERIK *looks at a map on the wall. It's hand made, with newspaper cuttings glued to a piece of white paper.*

ERIK. What's this?

TIASHA. My map. Where I was in the world.

ERIK *stares at the map.*

Erik . . . you still want me?

ERIK *sits on* TIASHA*'s bed, puts his head in his hands and massages it.*

Erik?

ERIK. Of course.

TIASHA. You said. Always.

ERIK. Yeah, I did, didn't I.

ERIK *fixes his eyes onto a point somewhere in the empty space in front of him.* TIASHA *sits next to him, looking ahead as well. But her face shows the issue has been settled. The wind opens the window.*

TIASHA. Windy. Is it always windy here?

ERIK. Almost.

TIASHA. Like it's pushing you somewhere.

ERIK *nods.* TIASHA *snuggles up to him.*

I am sorry for people in this hostel. They are free but they are not. They can go where they want, but where do they want to go when nothing is familiar.

ERIK *nods.*

ERIK. We should close the window.

Scene Seven

MILA *and* MARKO*'s flat.*

GAYLE *and* MARKO *kissing. Food and wine around them on the floor.*

GAYLE. Wait –

MARKO. No –

GAYLE (*giggles*). Hey, wait –

MARKO. I hate waiting.

GAYLE (*giggles again*). No. This. Is this desperation?

MARKO. If it is, I'll volunteer.

GAYLE. Because if it is, it might taste bitter afterwards.

MARKO. Bitter is a good solid taste. 'Bitter' is better than 'bland', than 'watery', and definitely better than 'nothing'.

GAYLE. I think 'nothing' is better than 'bitter'.

MARKO. Then you're missing out on a lot.

GAYLE. Am I?

MARKO. But I promise it won't be bitter.

They kiss.

GAYLE. I got turned down by an exhibition I worked three months for. I got yelled at by a beggar with green teeth whom I've almost stepped on. I got proposed to by a sixty-eight-year-old Sudanese refugee who shits in his pants when he forgets to take his medication. And now I'm about to sleep with a man I hardly know.

MARKO. See, a cherry on top.

She pulls away.

(*Sighs, but gently.*) Wanna talk about it?

GAYLE. In Wellington, I'd always walk a miserable day off.

MARKO. Well, granted, I'm not as exciting as a walk down Wellington High Street –

GAYLE *laughs.*

But . . . I'm 'Pick of the Day' in Deptford.

GAYLE *laughs. Then she turns sad again.*

GAYLE. When I've had a miserable day, I start intensely missing things. Sitting in cafés. That lovely wave-like pace of living where you can allow yourself to sit in cafés.

MARKO. Yeah. Four hour meals, that's us.

GAYLE. Knowing there will be familiar faces in particular cafés.

MARKO. Meeting with friends now and not next Thursday.

GAYLE. Riding a bike, not the tube.

MARKO. How easy it is to have a conversation with somebody on the tram or the bus. But hey, you're likely to see them again at some point.

GAYLE. Not like here.

MARKO. No. God forbid eye contact.

GAYLE. It's the fear, I think. Your eyelids are like blinds. They hide your frailty. Look up and you're a victim.

Pause. They look at each other. She breaks eye contact.

And this – (*Pointing to drinks and snacks.*) you rob a bank?

MARKO. I work three hundred hours a day at that bar!

GAYLE. Aha. Somehow I doubt this is your normal diet.

MARKO. Actually I enjoy a little caviar in the morning.

GAYLE. Come on, 'fess up.

MARKO. What, you don't believe me? (*Puts on an 'Ali G' voice*.) Is it because I is a Serb?

GAYLE *squints at him*. MILA *walks in*.

MILA. Oh . . . sorry. Interrupting.

GAYLE *pulls back*. MARKO *is annoyed*.

(*To* MARKO.) Well, I'm sorry, you should have your picnics in your bedroom.

MARKO. My room can fit a picnic or us. But not both.

MILA (*to* GAYLE). Hi, I'm Mila.

GAYLE. Gayle, nice to meet you.

MILA. Don't mind me. I've just popped in to change. Ooh, salmon.

She bends down and quickly puts together a sandwich.

You don't mind, do you? Very impressive . . .

MARKO. Mila, get lost.

MILA. Where d'you get the money for this?

GAYLE *looks at* MARKO *inquisitively*. MILA *realises she said something wrong*.

Sorry. Don't mind me. I'm on a total high. Mnme, mnmni, mnmno . . .

She goes out to change. MARKO *shrugs*.

GAYLE (*carefully*). Was there a woman?

MARKO. Ever? There were three! Okay, two.

GAYLE *smiles but she's not playing along*.

(*Admitting it*.) Mates were supposed to come visit from Belgrade. But they cancelled.

GAYLE. Classy mates.

MARKO. Yeah. I was going to impress them. But if I can, I'd rather impress you . . .

GAYLE *smiles*. MILA *comes back in wearing her nurse's uniform*.

. . . If she ever leaves.

MILA. I'm going, man!

GAYLE. You're a nurse.

MILA. Um . . . more of a babysitter really. For one-hundred-kilo-stone babies.

GAYLE doesn't understand.

I look after old people. In a home. Shit pay, they treat me like shit and there's a lot of actual shit involved. I'm a really good person.

GAYLE. But, Marko said you had a part in a play.

MILA. Oh, yeah. I'm playing a Russian hooker. Going against the cliché. It's actually really exciting.

GAYLE. That's great.

MILA. Yeah. You know, it's small, but it's, you know, an English crew which is important. You know, it's not like a Christmas show down at the Croatian community centre.

MARKO. You don't even know where that is.

MILA. Exactly. I keep telling him – integrate and rule!

They smile to each other, inadvertently making GAYLE *feel like an outsider.*

Anyway, I'm off. Not enough hours in the day here, have you noticed? I practise on the bus, people think I'm crazy. You're pretty. (*To* MARKO.) She's pretty.

She takes a sip of his wine. MARKO *pushes her off. There is a real intimacy about them.*

Bye.

She runs out.

MARKO. Mila.

GAYLE. And you are not . . .

MARKO. No.

GAYLE. Because . . .

MARKO. No 'because'. Just no.

GAYLE. She's going out with Erik?

MARKO. She's even got a wedding in mind.

GAYLE. Are you serious?

MARKO. Well . . . I don't know. On a bad day. Then she thinks she wants to settle down.

GAYLE. With him.

MARKO. Yeah, of all people. But there are days she's working and she's happy, so –

GAYLE. You don't like him.

MARKO. I . . . think . . . he is a destroyer.

GAYLE. Do you think there's compassion in him?

MARKO. Compassion? He fools around with war reports like they were video games.

GAYLE. And you don't think there's something behind that front?

MARKO. There's plenty, I'm sure. But I'm not sure if it's better or worse.

GAYLE is consumed with worry.

So, this help that you wanted from him . . . did you get it?

GAYLE. Um . . . yeah . . . He has so much experience with the war zones . . . particularly Balkans . . . You know he spent a better part of two years there . . .

MARKO. Right. So he . . . ?

GAYLE. Helps me . . . understand . . .

MARKO. I suppose he's got some stories to tell . . .

GAYLE gives him a trapped glance.

GAYLE. Yeah.

It seems like GAYLE is going to confide in MARKO. A split second and she decides against it.

MARKO. What?

GAYLE. I thought you were going to start impressing me . . .

MARKO. Oh, how could I forget! On your mark . . . Ready –

GAYLE (*laughing*). Go!

*

TIASHA is sitting in her hostel room putting together her map. Now it has another route on it, ERIK's course.

48

TIASHA. You know, between us two, we more or less went around whole world. And where we didn't go, we can go together. Or maybe, we have enough of world.

*

It's late at night in MILA *and* MARKO's *flat.* MARKO *is sitting, drinking the rest of the wine from the bottle. Music coming from the stereo.* MILA *appears in the room quietly. She watches him. He turns. He doesn't try to pretend.*

MILA. You okay?

Pause.

They're not coming.

MARKO *shakes his head.*

Visa?

MARKO. Turned down after all. They didn't serve the army.

MILA. I'm sorry.

MARKO. I really wanted to see them. I was really . . .

MILA (*Pauses*). I'm sure it would have been shit, though.

MARKO. Oh, yeah, for sure.

MILA. They would have made a mess of our place, maybe even get arrested –

MARKO. Probably charged with drug possession –

MILA. And embarrass you in front of the lovely foreign girlfriend.

MARKO. Piss off.

MILA. She . . . ? (*Motioning towards* MARKO's *room.*)

MARKO. Asleep.

MILA. Good?

MARKO. Lovely.

MILA (*teasing*). Aren't you afraid she's using you? Examining you for trauma?

MARKO. She's an artist, social work is just . . .

MILA. Well, that's reassuring. So what does she do, read them bedtime stories?

MARKO. Fuck if I know – takes them to Asda, shows them where to buy platanas, teaches them not to try to talk to the answering machines, you know, the important stuff.

MILA *laughs*.

I'll rot in hell. She's great.

MILA. How about open-mike night?

MARKO (*turning weary*). I got nervous, my English was shit, nothing was funny. Nobody laughed. It was painful.

MILA. But you're getting so good.

MARKO (*pointing to the food and drink*). Pathetic, ha? What a stupid, stupid, thing to do. Buy expensive food to – what – imitate success? They don't even like salmon.

MILA. I do. It blows up in your face but we'll eat like royalty the next few days. Cos, you went out on a spree! How could you afford –

MARKO. It's a crap life here, Mila.

MILA *sits next to him*.

MILA. Marko . . .

MARKO. It is. We're not welcome here. They were going to be here for a week. One week. And they would spend here in one week what they've been saving up for months. But they can't come here and spend money on overpriced entertainment and lousy food because they didn't serve the army.

MILA. That's not us. We are here.

MARKO. Nobody's happy with us being here. I mean, are we happy?

MILA. We're happy.

MARKO. Are we happier than home?

MILA. You're not thinking of going back, are you?

MARKO. I left saying, screw you! To come back with my tail between my legs . . . Now there's a formula for alcoholism. Besides, they just burnt down a mosque in Belgrade. Don't feel like rushing back.

MILA (*takes his face into her hands*). Marko, *gledaj me.*
[Look at me.] We'll be all right. We said – 'No Mood'. The
Mood sneaks in when we are off guard and shoots apathy in
our butts.

MARKO *smiles.*

We have fought it off before and we will do it again.

Pause.

We'll be okay. We have a plan. We will be okay.

*An intense moment. For a brief second it looks as though
they might kiss but they don't.*

Beat.

MARKO. I better go check on the foreign girlfriend.

He gets up and goes to his room.

*

MILA *is rehearsing her part. She is sitting on a barstool
again, this time wearing skimpy clothes – white, high-
heeled boots, a very short skirt, a tight top – her costume.
She has pointed a table lamp at herself to imitate a
spotlight. She is holding a script. She is singing a Russian
song, 'Ochi Chorneje'. She stops, coughs, does some voice
exercises. She mutters the other characters' lines quietly.
She sings and speaks in a Russian accent. Her voice is
seductive and her moves sexy.*

MILA. 'I know now, I understand that what's important about
our work – whether we act on the stage or write – isn't
fame, it isn't glory, it's none of those things I used to dream
of, it's simply the capacity to endure.'

*She starts humming the melody to the song. Whilst sitting
on the stool she begins to dance, like a beginning of a strip
act. She stops. She frowns, unhappy with what she did. She
thinks about it then.*

'Do you remember? Everything was so clear and warm, life
was so joyous, so innocent – and such feelings we had, like
delicate, exquisite flowers. Do you remember?'

She smiles as if she found the right code.

Scene Eight

Snapshots.

ERIK *appears.* MILA *is still on her chair, using moments between lines to choreograph her scene. She's excited and positive.*

MILA. You are right. It is all going well. It's ups and downs here, isn't it? It takes time.

ERIK. Yes. Yes, of course.

MILA. Sometimes nothing's right and I panic. But you know I'm not like that. We need space, both of us. Because we like freedom, even when we're together. That doesn't mean we're not together.

ERIK. Yes. Yes, of course. Don't be silly. It's all right.

*

TIASHA *appears in a separate space.* ERIK *is caught between them.*

TIASHA. Not Norway then? I don't like the cold but on the other hand, look, I would like to live here.

She produces a magazine photograph of a Norwegian landscape.

ERIK. Tiasha, let's slow down for a moment. There are things to consider.

TIASHA. Of course, I know. I'm just saying. So that you know. I think I like Norway.

ERIK (*irritably*). Norway is out of the question!

TIASHA. Okay. (*Pause.*) Why?

ERIK. All my friends are married with children. Children they made having soundless sex. They have dinners and discuss double glazing . . . They would hardly understand me. Me and you – not a fucking chance.

TIASHA (*quietly*). All right.

*

MILA. We'll always be unpredictable and open-minded. That's what we are like. And even if we were a more normal couple and had more stability. That doesn't mean we're becoming dull . . .

ERIK. You're way ahead of me.

MILA. In fact, I am. That's why I'm saying this. Because I'm thinking ahead.

ERIK. Life is about moments, Mila. It's a mistake to think you can stretch them into a constant.

MILA *produces a sound of excitement and exasperation, as if to say 'You're impossible'. She kisses* ERIK *quickly and runs off.*

*

TIASHA. Then London?

ERIK. We'll see.

TIASHA. I don't think I like London. You do, don't you?

ERIK (*irritably*). I don't know, Tiasha. Not as much as I used to . . .

TIASHA (*withdrawing*). Oh. Yes. No.

ERIK. I mean, we'll talk about it. I have to go now.

TIASHA. Can I come?

ERIK. No! No, it's . . . I can't take you along.

TIASHA. Okay.

ERIK *leaves.*

I don't like it here. Airplanes and sirens all the time. Sounds the same like the war.

*

GAYLE *is looking at* TIASHA*'s map on the wall. There are two trajectories marked in different colours. One is* TIASHA*'s and the other is* ERIK*'s.* TIASHA *leaves.*

GAYLE. See. I bet this would win the bloody Turner Prize in a second. Of course, it should be a bit more interactive. Maybe if you press a particular country and a video of a massacre pops out. (*Pause.*) You know how people spend years saving money to go travelling.

She gives a little bitter laugh.

I shouldn't be showing you this. I shouldn't be telling you this. It's so highly unprofessional of me. But you listen. And you look me in the eyes. You know, she looked at my boxes and she said, there is nothing nice at the bottom of any box. I suppose she was right. She says, he still has the same heart and that's all that matters. (*She puts her finger on Belgrade.*) Will you take me to Belgrade one time? Be-o-grad. White city. Beautiful.

Music.

Darkness.

Sound of wind.

Scene Nine

MICHI*'s bar.*

MILA *is sitting on a barstool singing a heavy, sad song.* MARKO *and* ERIK *are sitting having drinks. Gloom, all around.*

MICHI (*entering*). Oho! What's with her? Change of policy? I could do with more of that. Good, Mila, good. Depressing but can be used.

She doesn't pay attention.

So! Where is all the paparazzi?

MARKO. Hey, Michi, leave her. She had a tough night.

ERIK *puts the same music on the stereo.*

ERIK (*to* MILA). Come here. (*He takes her to dance.*)

MILA *(to* ERIK). You haven't said much.

ERIK. I think there's no reason to get worked up.

MARKO (*to* MICHI). It didn't go so well.

MICHI. What? Why?

MILA. I didn't stick to the plan, that's why. The plan was – have faith, work hard and triumph. No shortcuts, no digressions.

MICHI. I don't understand.

MILA. The plan was musicals. Ever since I was eight years old, that was the plan.

MICHI. Yes, yes, 'story of my life' not so interesting right now.

MILA hides her face in ERIK*'s chest.* ERIK *starts dancing playfully, wanting to turn the situation into a joke.*

MARKO. She had a part of a Russian prostitute.

MICHI. Yes?

MARKO. Which is in itself terribly rewarding.

MICHI. Why?

MARKO. Well, you know, it's a stereotype.

MICHI. Of what?

MARKO. Of a Russian prostitute. It's always the same.

MICHI has lost him.

Doesn't matter. (*To* MILA.) I thought it was supposed to be a proper part, with lines and all.

MILA. It was.

MARKO. But then . . .

MILA. Lines got cut, day by day.

MARKO. Right, but there was a monologue . . .

MILA. Yesterday there was a monologue. It was taken from Chekhov, man! Not that they'd be fit to clean Chekhov's boots! So, today, the wanker –

MARKO. The director.

MILA. – decided to cut the whole monologue out. And I was left with no lines.

MICHI. No talking?

ERIK. Arguably, Russian hookers are not really famous for talking.

MICHI agrees and MILA *looks at* ERIK*, genuinely surprised at his comment.* MILA *wants to break away from* ERIK*, but he insists on continuing to dance, won't let her go.*

MILA. Let go of me.

He laughs but is still holding on to her. MARKO *approaches as* MILA *breaks off and he stands in between them. He is not confrontational, but there is something paternal about his behavior.*

MARKO. Hey, lay off.

ERIK *comes close to starting a physical fight.*

Erik, man, what's with you?

ERIK *gives up. Again, his superiority.*

ERIK. Yeah.

ERIK *stays dancing on his own with a glass in his hand.* MILA *goes over to the bar and lights a cigarette.*

MARKO. Hey, don't.

MILA. What? I'll grow another head in a while with the stuff we eat here, but I'm not gonna smoke? (*To* MICHI.) The wanker wanted moaning. My acting task was to moan.

MICHI. Let's hear.

MILA (*dismissing his proposal*). Visceral. He wanted visceral. I swear, if anybody so much as mentions 'visceral' to me ever again, as if they had any idea what it was. He wanted me to be a 'geyser of visceral eastern sexual charge'.

MICHI (*laughs*). A geyser? I like him. You want we go say 'Hello'?

MILA. No, I don't, why would I want – Oh, no. No, no, no. We are not going to say 'Hello'. We are staying completely out if it.

MICHI (*laughs*). Relax. I am joking. What do you think, Michi is Italian mafia? I want to lighten this up a little, but seems devil took away the joke.

ERIK. It would be quite fun to see the Oxford Ginger 'ra-*ther*' open his doors to Michi.

MILA (*reprehending*). Come on.

ERIK. Lighten up. It's not the end of the world.

MARKO. You're drunk.

MILA. All the time, all the time I felt like they keep expecting me to do something unpredictable and wild, preferably sexual. Like I was some kind of an exotic eastern specimen, that's, you know, got a trauma but shags like an animal. That's what turns men on. So depressing.

ERIK. So dramatic, dear. You took your clothes off, so what?

MICHI (*suddenly turning serious*). Hang on. Who took what where?

ERIK. She did. She lost the lines and the clothes.

MICHI. You strip? For real?

MILA. It was acting.

MICHI. Don't you mess me, did you have clothes off or clothes on?

Silence.

How much?

Silence.

All?

Silence. MICHI *begins to puff in anger.*

Well, beautiful. Isn't it? Michi offers you good money to strip for clients who can appreciate, in a place which is meant for that, you spit on Michi with detest. That director pay you shit money in shit theatre in zone fifty-six, no one ever come to see and what kind of place is theatre to do strip and, somehow, you do it?!

MILA *is unprepared. She looks at* MARKO *and* ERIK *for help.*

ERIK (*carelessly*). He's got a point.

MARKO. You're being very supportive tonight, aren't you?

ERIK. Which of the signals did she miss?!

MILA. Michi . . . I didn't want to strip, I don't want to do that. I thought, I don't know what I thought, it all happened so fast.

ERIK. You thought you'd strip on the off chance that somehow miraculously it hits the mark and the right people miraculously happen to see it and it transfers to the West End you're the talk of the town –

MILA. What?

MARKO. She stripped because they manipulated her to think it's a skill.

ERIK. You took a risk, deal with it.

MILA *is shaken*.

MARKO. Maybe give her a few minutes to get over it? (*To* MILA.) Hey, you'll be okay. It will be fine.

ERIK. It is fine. Your stripping was the best bit. I can't remember when I had more fun in theatre.

MILA. Watching your girlfriend strip?

ERIK. Yeah!

MILA. You're a sick man.

ERIK. I thought you would be pleased, someone as open-minded as you, to hear me say I don't mind dating a stripper.

MILA. I am not a stripper!

MICHI. Stripper – stripper –

ERIK. So I'm saying hypothetically.

MILA. But you wouldn't marry a stripper?

ERIK. What's that got to do with it?

MILA. I think it's amazing how men pretend to be free of prejudice before they actually start picking out someone to marry.

ERIK. I couldn't give an answer to that.

MILA. Why not?

ERIK. Because nothing could be further from my mind than marriage.

Beat.

MICHI. Marry stripper, date stripper, blah, blah. One thing is sure – no stripper in here. I carry you like drop of water because you announce your tall standards like a trumpet. And then you turn around and stab me in back.

GAYLE *walks in with a smile on her face but it doesn't last long*.

GAYLE. Hey.

She is barely acknowledged. ERIK *looks at her and is hardly pleased to see her here.* MARKO *smiles, goes to greet her but his attention is clearly elsewhere.*

MILA. You carry me 'like a drop of water'?!

MARKO (*to* GAYLE). Hey.

GAYLE. What's –

MARKO *offers her a seat and starts pouring her a drink.*

MARKO (*trying to arbitrate*). Mila, come down.

MILA. You must be joking!

MICHI. I do! Because I care about my people. I could get into lot of trouble for giving you work. You think I don't know you? If you take this seriously, you could have good life here. But no, because you despise this. This is temporary stop before you are star. Wake up! This is real life and not your bubble-soap dream. On the top of that, I give you liberty to protest because I like you. People in your situation shut up and work. Bloody Balkan cheek!

MILA. I'm grateful for the risk you're taking, but let's not forget you pay me half of what a singer would make somewhere else!

MARKO. Mila, that's enough.

MICHI. Maybe you want to try somewhere else then? Maybe you want to try pick some cockle?

Beat. MICHI*'s phone rings.*

No, I don't think so. I should know better from first day. You can smell scabby donkey across seven hills. (*Into the phone.*) Roman, my friend, what can I do for you?

He goes. MILA *is on the verge of crying. She looks at* ERIK, *expecting support.*

ERIK. You hurt the man.

MARKO *observes* ERIK *and is getting increasingly annoyed.* ERIK *is clearly provoking them.*

MILA (*to* GAYLE). Hey, Gayle.

GAYLE. Hey. Hi. How did –

But MILA *cuts her off, turning to* ERIK, *her tone really pissed off.*

MILA. And what is your problem?

ERIK. My problem?

MILA. Yeah. Did I do something to you?

ERIK. I don't know what you mean.

MILA. I mean, you're acting like a jerk.

ERIK. Thanks.

Silence. ERIK's *expression changes. His face is dark.* MILA *looks anxious as if waiting for a verdict.*

MILA. Okay, I'm sorry.

ERIK. I'm tired.

ERIK *gets up, puts some money on the counter.*

MARKO. Keep it.

ERIK *ignores him and pushes the money closer to* MARKO.

I said, keep it.

MILA. I said I was sorry.

MARKO. Why are you sorry?!

MILA. Marko, come on . . .

MARKO (*to* ERIK). Can you at least pretend to be kind, for one night?

Startled by MARKO's *forcefulness, everyone looks at him, speechless.*

Can't you see she could use some understanding?

ERIK. I thought, with so much coming from you, she might overdose.

MARKO. Fuck you!

MILA. Don't . . .

MARKO. Don't what? Arrogant bastard who treats you like shit –

ERIK *laughs.* GAYLE *takes a shot at pacifying* MARKO.

GAYLE. Hey, maybe we should –

MARKO. What is funny?

ERIK *looks at each of them, as if giving himself time to drop the subject.* GAYLE *terrified,* MILA *puzzled,* MARKO *fuming. But what the hell . . .*

ERIK. You, your moral highness. You are funny.

A tense moment.

Your capacity to pass judgment is extraordinary considering you got here cashing in on your dad's favours and now you work for this Balkan Mafioso and get generously tipped by half of the Eastern European mafia.

MARKO *and* MILA *are quite unprepared for this. They're both about to speak, but* ERIK *got himself going.*

MILA. They are not criminals!

ERIK. What are they?

MILA. . . . Okay, they are. But, you don't understand how things are where we come from. It's not that simple.

ERIK. Either they break the law or they don't. Which is it?

MILA. Well, I suppose then, yes, but . . .

ERIK. But somehow, that is okay. That we can turn a blind eye to. You spread around the world with that ridiculous cult of honour and reputation! And I'm arrogant!

MARKO. Look, man, you've obviously got issues with Balkan and stuff. Which, you know, we all understand.

ERIK. You don't wanna patronise me.

MARKO. You threatening me?

ERIK (*to* MILA). And you've been to more fetish clubs than you can count –

MARKO. With you!

ERIK. With me. But she liked it. And now suddenly her purity is bruised.

MILA *is taking all of this in, sensing there is something about* ERIK *that's much more destructive than usual.*

MILA. Erik, what the hell's going on?

ERIK. Do you even know why she's living with you? Do you know it makes her feel defiant and fucking controversial? A nice Croatian girl shacking up with a Serbian boy? What would they say to that back home? (*To* GAYLE.) My God, you must feel like an outsider. (*To* MILA.) And she doesn't even know that she hit the jackpot!

MARKO *and* MILA *stare at* ERIK. *They have no idea where this is going.*

Night shifts, I told you, fascinating stuff comes out when you look into the right places.

MILA. What are you talking about?

ERIK (*to* MARKO). Were you ever going to tell her what your daddy does?

MARKO *stares at him in disbelief.*

MILA. What?

ERIK. You know, his dad, big-shot commie. Sad thing with those guys . . . Times change, there's a war, there's democracy. Once they were top of the world, now they're just forgotten old wrecks.

MARKO*'s face is stern and grim. He knows what's coming, and knows there's no way out.*

Tragic, really. The way myths crumble and the living corpses are left behind.

MILA. We know that.

ERIK. No, we don't. We don't know that. We believe that, because that's what he tells us. What he doesn't tell us is that there is another option. When there's a war, you see, there are people who volunteer.

MILA. Wh . . . I don't understand.

ERIK. And they do what they have to do. In a war. When the war's over, they don't sit around in pyjamas waiting for PTSD to kick in. No. They embrace transition, privatising, wheeling and dealing. They end up owning an insurance company. They make a fortune, insuring, by and large, former war-buddies, now fellow-businessmen. They wear expensive suits and drive an Audi but what they don't do is talk about raping women or gutting old men because, well, that would just be in poor taste. (*Pause.*) And they have a son who can mix cocktails. Because they own a bloody cocktail bar on a beach!

MILA *looks at* MARKO *hopefully.* GAYLE *too.* MARKO *is silent.* ERIK *looks worn out. He is not really sure why he did this, tension relief maybe, but not much relief has come out of it.* MICHI *has come back in and is trying to make sense of the situation.*

MILA. Marko . . .

MICHI. What, is this a funeral?

MARKO (*to* MILA). That has nothing to do with me. That's my dad. More or less. That is why I left. I can't . . . (*He shrugs, defeated.*)

MICHI. Ah, the truth. Fancy that.

GAYLE. Marko . . .

ERIK. Did you think it would never come out?

MARKO *pauses for a second, he bites his lip as if trying to prevent the words from coming out, then:*

MARKO. Did you think Tiasha would never come out?

GAYLE (*panicking*). Marko, don't.

MILA. What – who?

ERIK *looks at* MARKO *in terror. Then he resigns. That is, in fact, where he was aiming to end up.*

ERIK. So. You know.

MILA. Know what?

MARKO *looks at* GAYLE *who is staring at him, horrified. He looks at her with remorse, but is not turning back now.*

Know what?!

Pause. Massive tension. ERIK *sits down on the first available chair, or the floor even.*

ERIK *begins to cry.*

Who the fuck is Tiasha?

Darkness.

Music.

Scene Ten

Snapshots.

A street. The wind. Yellow lights. GAYLE *intercepts* ERIK.

GAYLE. I shouldn't have told him. I'm sorry.

ERIK. You're not sworn to secrecy to me.

GAYLE. I'm not like that.

> ERIK *waves his hand as if to say it didn't matter. He makes to leave.*

You can't leave her.

ERIK. I can't help her.

> *Pause.*

GAYLE. I should have known. I should have know that you'd be like that . . .

> *She breaks. She cries.* ERIK *can't believe there's more.*

ERIK. Look . . .

GAYLE. I should have known he'd use me to help Mila.

ERIK. Serbs can't be trusted. Apparently. Says Mila. I don't think she means Marko, though.

GAYLE. Nor can Norwegians.

ERIK. I'm sure she would agree with you. Look, he's just weak.

GAYLE. How is that an excuse?

ERIK. It's not. Then again, if people weren't weak, there wouldn't be half as much fun in the world.

*

MICHI. So, you blow it.

MARKO. I didn't mean it.

MICHI. Way to hell is paved with good intentions. Women – always trouble. You better come work with Michi. I have half the capital so far.

MARKO. She'll never forgive me.

MICHI. Which one?

*

ERIK. Look . . . I'm not much of a bargain. She'll be better off without me.

GAYLE. You're a coward.

GAYLE *disappears into the dark.*

*

TIASHA. My grandfather told me a story when I was little. It is about Bird King. Bird King lived in our country many centuries ago. People were working hard but country was poor and people were weak. They would come home in the night and weep. The Bird King was sorry. He spoke to Yanesh, the smartest of the people, and he said: I can help you. I can divide your life into life of body and life of heart. If body and heart have separate lives, then body can work hard and not feel grief. Yanesh said: But what will happen to the heart? The heart, said the Bird King, you give to somebody who is dear to you to keep. Until you have done your work, sowed and reaped and picked and plucked and plant and plowed. But what about those who have not yet found anyone so dear. The Bird King said, I will keep their hearts until they do. And so it was. The people worked much better with their hearts in safekeeping and the country was becoming richer and more food was put on the table. And everybody was happy.

*

MICHI*'s bar lights up.* MARTA *is sweeping the floor.* ERIK *is carrying a suitcase.*

MARTA. Nobody here. Nobody here at this time.

ERIK. Oh, right.

MARTA. You don't know that?

ERIK. I thought maybe . . . (*Pause.*) My God, this is a dump.

MARTA. You don't know dumps.

ERIK. Actually, I do.

MARTA. Oh, yes. You die in Bosna.

ERIK. You know about that?

MARTA. I think everybody know.

ERIK. I suppose it's a good story.

MARTA. My husband die in Bosna. (*Pause*.) But he stay dead.

ERIK. I'm sorry.

MARTA. No why. He was rubbish. But still, much larger rubbish still living.

ERIK. True.

MARTA. You run away?

ERIK. I need a break.

MARTA. You afraid . . .

ERIK. I'm not afraid. Nothing can happen that hasn't happened before.

MARTA. To stay, I mean. Run away always hurt someone.

ERIK. I don't want to hurt anyone. Sometimes people do things, bad things because . . . For all kinds of reasons that can't be helped.

MARTA. People do bad things because they can.

Pause.

ERIK. I have to get going. Tell Michi I said hi and see you in a while.

MARTA. You take care. You are not cat with nine life.

Music.

Sound of rain.

Scene Eleven

A restaurant.

A tiny table with a white tablecloth. A lean tall vase with a single red flower.

TIASHA *and* MILA *are sitting at the table*. TIASHA *is calm and* MILA *visibly nervous*.

MILA. We haven't really been introduced.

MILA *extends her hand*. TIASHA *takes it. Their handshake across the table is almost grotesque*.

Mila.

TIASHA. Tiasha.

Pause. MILA *watches* TIASHA *as if she were inspecting her for some rare signs of difference, something visible that distinguishes her from all the women in the world. She has a full awareness of both their bodies and the space between them.* TIASHA *seems perfectly careless. It's not that she feels comfortable in this place where she does not, at all, belong. It's simply that to her it's no more than a stop on the way, therefore has nothing frightening about it.*

MILA. Did you have trouble finding this place?

TIASHA. No. Gayle gave me A-Z. I walk and find everything.

MILA. You walked?

TIASHA. Yes.

MILA. People don't walk in London.

TIASHA. Why not?

MILA. Because they don't have time.

TIASHA. I have plenty.

MILA. So you do. (*Pause.*) But you shouldn't walk at night. It's dangerous. People get mugged, or raped even . . . (*Stops. Realises who she is talking to. Pause.*) I . . . Would you like to order?

TIASHA. I'm not really hungry.

MILA. Yes. All right. Just drinks then.

TIASHA. Yes.

MILA. Just as well. Never can fit the plates properly on these tables. I never could understand, why is it so hard to put proper-sized tables in restaurants. Extra large prices – no problem! But even a medium-sized table that is too much to ask. You know, I've been to quite a few restaurants, and I've left a shit load of money there and I haven't once, not once, sat at a proper-sized table where the person next to me is not breathing down my neck!

Pause. TIASHA *is not responding.*

He is gone, you do know that?

TIASHA. Yes.

MILA. And . . . Look, it's nice of you to come. I mean, I know you didn't have to. I mean, I always thought, it's not the other woman that a woman should have a problem with. It's the man, isn't it? But what do you do when the man vanishes? And I'm not even sure which one of us is the other woman.

TIASHA *listens to* MILA *carefully, with full attention, but one can't see any distinct reaction on her face.*

So frustrating, none of the standard explanations apply because he's so . . . And you're so . . . (*Stops. She struggles to find words. She gives up.*) Has he been in touch with you?

TIASHA. No.

MILA. Are you . . . What have you . . . Why are you here?

TIASHA. Sorry?

MILA. No, I'm sorry, but I just don't understand. Everything was fine and then you showed up and everything seems to have gone to hell.

TIASHA. I'm sorry.

MILA. Oh, God, I hate the past. Hate it, hate it, hate it. Nothing good ever comes from it. Just bad memories and demons.

Pause.

TIASHA. I think I don't know what you want to know.

MILA. I want to know what it was like between you two. Is it because you were with him when he got shot that he's still so affected by you, and do you want him for the papers and –

TIASHA. I got papers.

MILA. What?

TIASHA. My papers are all right. They came. I can stay.

MILA. You can stay?!

TIASHA. Yes.

MILA. So soon? It's been like six months!

TIASHA *shrugs.*

68

Pause.

MILA *is distraught: 'How does one get through to this woman?!'*

TIASHA. I don't know where he is. I don't know what is happened to him. I think this city is not very good for people. He can't look me in the eyes. I thought perhaps it is something he is ashamed of. I thought, he doesn't need to be ashamed of anything, I don't mind whatever he is done. But then I see, nobody looks anybody in the eyes. Is everyone here ashamed? I don't want him for the papers. It's other way around. I want papers to be with him.

MILA. But he left you. He left you twice. He left me. He left me wondering a million times before.

TIASHA. It's not easy for him. He doesn't do that because he likes it.

MILA. No, that's wrong. He hurts us and we feel sorry for his pain. You know when you can't understand what goes on in someone's head that doesn't necessarily mean that's mysterious and complex and meta-fucking-physical. Maybe it's just bollocks. Obscure bollocks.

TIASHA. I think it must be very difficult for you. When you so need simple explanation, it will be difficult for you to be in peace. (*Pause.*) If I try to find simple explanation why people do things they did to me, I go crazy. Sometimes there are too much things that . . . (*She uses her hands to explain.*) around your instinct and you can't breathe. I think it's not good to wait for other people words. You find your own. Here. (*She puts her palm on her stomach.*)

*

MICHI *is sitting at the bar. The bar is empty, the lights are dim. He is on the phone, silent. Then he puts the receiver down and lights a cigarette.*

MICHI (*exhaling the smoke heavily*). Bloody fucking lump. Michi, you should know by now. It's not going anywhere, it is here forever. Bloody thing is scratching your throat. You can't swallow, you can't spit out. You think it will go away one day when you do this or when you do that, when you make big, earn money, go away, come back. But no. On the end you see it's not going away. Lump is life. Best chance, keep it not to grow. Your devil. Doesn't get much better than just keep him happy and calm. Sooner you learn, better. Fifty-six years old, Michi, and you still forget.

*

TIASHA *and* MILA *are standing in the street. Yellow lights. Wind.*

TIASHA. I like the river. It looks like it has power but doesn't have to use it.

MILA. I'll walk with you for a bit, if that's all right.

TIASHA. Yes.

MILA. I used to always walk in Zagreb. Now I just run all the time.

TIASHA. I wasn't allowed to walk for years.

Pause.

MILA. I'm so exhausted, you know, of trying to . . . It's like trying to win him over. Then I wonder, why am I trying to do that? He always crossed the street without looking to see where I was. Like . . . he was never with me.

TIASHA. I think he must care about you, in some way. He wouldn't be gone if that isn't so.

MILA *considers. She smiles. She could cry.*

MILA. I don't think that's my kind of caring.

TIASHA. I understand.

Pause.

MILA. I have to go to work. (*Pause.*) You will wait for him?

TIASHA. Yes.

They smile at each other. MILA *slowly walks away.*

A great fire came and burnt the trees. And with them, the castle of Bird King. So the Bird King and his birds had to fly away. They took with them all the hearts they were keeping. But the fire burnt their eyes and they were blind. And they could never find their way back. Most of the people were left without their hearts.

Pause.

I only had strength for everything because I gave him my heart to keep and I lived with my body. But now I need it back.

Pause.

It's simple like that. He has my heart. Nothing I can do about that.

MILA. I hope he knows.

TIASHA. He does.

Scene Twelve

Snapshots.

MICHI*'s bar.*

MICHI *is sitting, smoking his Davidoffs. He exhales the smoke with great heaviness. He looks very serious.*

MARKO *comes in.*

MARKO. What's up?

MICHI. Where's Mila?

MARKO. I don't know. We don't live together any more, remember.

MICHI. She can't let go because she is stubborn, not because she is hurt.

MARKO. Yeah. Well . . . I think she's at work. Actually, she should have been here already. What is this, are we closed?

MICHI. Yes.

MARKO. How come, on a Thursday?

MICHI. I will have to rethink our policy.

MARKO. Again?

MICHI. And in between time, I will have to let you go. You and Mila.

MARKO. What?!

MICHI. Yes. The big wave . . . I jumped but I suppose I slide off.

MARKO. I don't understand.

*

MILA *stumbles in the street, pressing her hands on a bleeding spot around her left kidney. She drops to the floor. She is in shock.*

MILA. Wait. Wait, wait. It's going to be all right. It's nothing.

She looks at her hands, covered in blood.

*

MICHI. It was a bad investment. To double the money.

MARKO. What kind of investment?

MICHI. You are not partner, remember? You are staff. You don't get to know what kind of investment.

MARKO. Michi –

MICHI. No Michi. That is how it is.

MARKO. So, you are closing.

MICHI. Only temporary. Until I / rethink my policy.

MARKO (*interrupting*). Rethink your policy. And you'll just fire us?

MICHI. I am not your fairy good mother.

Pause. MARKO *is trying to absorb the weight of this information.*

There is one club in East London. Clarence, manager, very good friend of mine. Maybe take you.

MARKO. Right.

*

MILA. It's nothing. It's just a cut. It'll be all right. (*Pause.*) Mama! That's right. *Nazvat ću mamu. Sve će bit okej.* [I'll call Mama. It'll be okay.] Mama.

With her hands shaking, she takes her mobile out of a pocket in her uniform and dials. She misdials.

Shit. Concentrate.

She dials again. A voice is heard from the phone: 'You have insufficient credit . . .'

Fuck you!

She drops the phone and cries.

(*Quietly.*) Help.

*

MARKO. I never thought something like that could happen to you.

MICHI. Good thing about life – just when you think it is becoming dull, there is always twist.

MARKO. And what about Mila?

Scene Thirteen

The hostel, GAYLE*'s office.*

MICHI*'s bar.*

An airport lounge.

To the left is GAYLE*'s desk and two chairs. A couple of plastic airport lounge chairs and a television set are in the centre. The counter of* MICHI*'s bar is to the right.*

GAYLE *is sorting out some papers.* MARKO *walks in.*
TIASHA*'s map is hanging from the wall next to* GAYLE*'s desk.*

MARKO. I didn't call. I thought . . .

GAYLE. I thought you might get in touch.

MARKO. I went to Brixton. To your house . . .

GAYLE. I moved. Closer to work.

MARKO. This work?

GAYLE. Yes, this is my work. (*Pause.*) Come in. Have a seat.

He does so.

Coffee?

MILA *enters the airport lounge carrying some hand baggage. She sits down on one of the chairs.*

MARKO. Yes, please.

MICHI (*enters the bar. On the phone, as usual*). Yes. No. Twice already I have to fire people you send me. One time, doorman, I would go better off with goldfish at my door. Second time, barman, steal off me every time I look the other side. No. I don't care what you think. To think is to know shit.

GAYLE (*to* MARKO). Of course. You never turn down drinks . . . or food.

MARKO. Countries less privileged. We always stock up, like camels. Never know when you're gonna run out.

GAYLE. Good to see you're still funny.

Beat.

Yes. How is Mila taking it?

MARKO. You know that home she worked at. She was on a night shift. A couple of guys came in through the window, burgled a few of those grannies. She walked in on them, one of them stabbed her.

GAYLE. Oh, my God!

MILA *is sitting in the airport lounge with her hand luggage next to her.* MARKO *comes over carrying two cups of coffee.* MILA *takes a bottle of pills from her handbag and swallows one with coffee.*

MARKO. You should have talked to someone. Professional, I mean.

MILA. I'm a child of communism, I don't believe in paying for advice. That, and I'm broke.

MARKO. There's victim support. It's for free.

MILA. Yeah, and imagine how good they are.

MARKO *laughs.*

Pause.

MARKO. What if you just go home for a while? Ha? Get well and come back.

MILA. Marko, I'm thirty. I've got a ruptured spleen. I can't dance. I've lost one job and the other . . . Well, I can't face going to that place, no therapy will help there. Man, they weren't old enough to carry a condom, let alone a knife.

MARKO. But hey, dancing with a ruptured spleen – I see performance art festivals killing for you.

MILA (*smiles*). In Croatia at least I can pretend I've come back with a vast worldly experience and teach or something. I'll be a tragic heroine. I'll get a piece in *Cosmo* about me. (*Pause*.) I'll recycle some of the old boyfriends.

MARKO. Hey, it's just this moment. It's a phase. Because of everything –

MILA. Actually – I miss home. I really do. I miss the feel of it. This doesn't feel like home. Because it's not. It's nobody's home. So nobody cares for it.

MARKO *turns back to* GAYLE.

GAYLE (*to* MARKO). She's right.

MARKO. She feels guilty.

GAYLE. She shouldn't. If anyone should feel guilty, it's me.

MARKO. That's not true.

GAYLE. Oh, yes, it is. I should have been focused. I should have known how horribly wrong it would go.

MARKO. She would have found him.

GAYLE. But I wouldn't feel responsible then. (*Pause*.) And you know something else – I thought it was incredibly intriguing, their case. That bloody map, I had a whole exhibition in mind, inspired by her. It was going to be called – 'The Silk Route'.

MARKO *is silent*.

MILA (*to* MARKO). And you were right. I have grown out of the anonymity phase. Being a smudge in the crowd can wear out.

GAYLE (*to* MARKO). You're appalled, aren't you?

MARKO. No, I . . .

GAYLE. Don't worry, so am I.

MARKO. I'm not. If you can make a piece of art out of somebody's pain, it's –

GAYLE. I've taken a full-time job here.

Beat. MARKO *is astonished.*

Which is really quite funny –

MARKO. Gayle –

GAYLE. I mean, considering my sunny disposition. But it's real.

MILA. We struggle for this great life that will begin one day and meanwhile the actual life is still on pause. I'm sick of that.

MICHI (*on the phone*). No, I will not wait more. I don't need a singer, I have a singer. No, not like Mila, what you think singer like Mila grows on trees, she has diploma for singing. (*Pause.*) No, she is gone.

ERIK *and* TIASHA *appear on opposite sides of the stage.* TIASHA *seems somehow hardened. They look at each other. They stand there, looking at each other.* TIASHA *sits next to* MILA, *but she is somewhere else. Maybe in a different airport. Sitting, waiting.*

MARKO. What if I go with you?

MILA. Are you crazy? I go off to the west and the best I can come back with is a Serb?

MARKO. It was a system of elimination, though.

A tender smile.

GAYLE. Everyone should be issued a Visa to come here. Not these poor things that ran to save their lives, but everyone who's come here with big dreams. I don't know, say three years. That's a fair length.

MICHI (*on the phone*). It's not charity I do here. I don't want another bloody lazy compatriot. Get me a Filipino or something, someone with some bloody work habits.

GAYLE. Whoever's not made it in that slot should bugger the hell out of here. Make room, let some air in. I swear this city will eventually sink with all these worn-out dreams holding by their teeth.

MARKO. Gayle –

GAYLE (*she raises her voice*). If it hasn't happened in ten years, it's never gonna happen. Snap out of it, people! I swear, if I ever have to talk to another fifty-year-old, grey-haired actor still auditioning daily . . . Or, if I ever have to talk about feminism with a crazy ageing . . . hippy . . . performance artist . . . dressed in rags . . . (*She stops herself.*) Of course you don't feel the same because it's worked out for you. I saw your name in the comedy listings. In *Time Out*.

MARKO. I'm sorry.

MILA. It's not your fault. I know.

MARKO (*to* GAYLE). It's only a little gig.

GAYLE (*shrugs*). Yeah, well . . .

MARKO. Look, Gayle, I didn't mean to . . . It just turned out that way . . .

GAYLE. It always turns out that way. For me.

MILA*'s mobile rings*.

MILA. Last call on the British phone. Must be the Queen. She'd like me to reconsider. (*Into the phone.*) Halo? Yes? Speaking. (*Pause.*) Yes.

MILA *puts the phone down and stares into the emptiness*.

It's Erik.

MARKO. Really? Where is he?

MILA. He's dead.

TIASHA *gets up and goes to* MICHI. *She sits beside him at the bar*.

MARTA *enters, sweeping the floor across the stage. Everyone observes her. It seems that for the first time they actually acknowledge her presence*.

TIASHA. You should pay her more.

MICHI. I pay her enough.

TIASHA. She's an old woman.

MARTA *walks over to where* MILA *is sitting. She turns on the television. CNN. In a characteristic CNN style, there is a report about* ERIK*'s death. Shots of street fights in Baghdad followed by* ERIK*'s head shot. It runs on mute*.

Everyone turns to watch the report. Except for TIASHA.

(*To* MICHI.) I need two thousand Euro.

MARTA *goes over to where* ERIK *is sitting*.

MARTA (*to* ERIK). Do you have a cigarette?

ERIK *offers her a packet*. MARTA *lights a cigarette. She points to the place beside him. He nods. She sits next to him. Exhales*.

MICHI (*to* TIASHA). Why?

TIASHA. For expenses.

MARKO (*to* GAYLE). She left her map?

GAYLE. Yes.

MARKO. That's odd. What are you going to do with it?

GAYLE. Keep it as a reminder. Of how I screwed up. And . . . of how I was engaged. Which made me feel good.

MICHI (*to* TIASHA). For when?

TIASHA. Tomorrow.

MICHI. Tomorrow?

TIASHA. Yes. I go tomorrow.

MICHI. I thought you wouldn't go until next month.

TIASHA. Change of plan.

MICHI. What change?

TIASHA. I just talked to Roman. He thinks as soon as possible I should go. Clarence needs more girls.

MICHI. What is the rush?

TIASHA. Clarence has a new club opening. Strictly members only. But for them – unlimited offer.

MICHI. But there is mess again in Kosovo. We should stay out of it.

TIASHA. Mess is when you do things.

MARKO *runs his fingers across the map*.

MARKO (*to* GAYLE). Erik told me all these stories about Bosna. He could tell a story, you know. I used some of them, some of the worst ones, for an act. That's the one that got me the gig.

GAYLE. Congratulations.

ERIK (*to* MARTA). The apple comes from California. Somebody picked it, God knows how long ago, and loaded it into a box and onto a truck. Then drove it to the airport, put it on a plane and shipped it over to Baghdad. Quite a long journey, I'd say. Then they unloaded them, unpacked them and served them to us. Perfection, I thought. Like the apple in *Snow White*. Perfectly red and shiny. I put it on my night table, the only beautiful thing around. The only thing that makes sense.

MARKO (*to* GAYLE). I'm going to Norway. For the funeral.

MICHI (*to* TIASHA). You will get yourself killed.

GAYLE (*to* MARKO). To pay your respects? Funny how people wait until the funeral to do that.

TIASHA (*to* MICHI). Michi, don't worry about me.

MARKO (*to* GAYLE). It's a phase. You know that. It's how we live here, in phases –

GAYLE. I'm sure that cheers Mila up – that's just a phase when you get stabbed. Or Erik – a phase when you get killed. Again.

MARKO. Come with me to Norway.

GAYLE. I'm sorry?

MARKO. I know you resent me, but . . . come with me.

MICHI (*to* TIASHA). I worry. I worry about both of us. (*Pause.*) It is not courage, what you do. It is reckless.

TIASHA. It is neither.

MICHI. This is no job for pretty young woman.

TIASHA. Washing toilets or old people bums is no job for pretty young women but they do it.

MICHI. Okay. You can't take a compliment.

TIASHA. Michi, we have a deal, do we not? I told you many times, don't try to get in my head.

MICHI. All right. Here. (*Handing her the money.*) When will you come back?

TIASHA. I don't know. Three weeks probably. I will call you to let you know. There should be two girls.

GAYLE (*to* MARKO). You think it will absolve you of guilt?

MARKO. You could look at it as homage, rather than exploitation.

GAYLE. Yes, you could.

MARKO. I mean, so could you.

GAYLE *nods, but she obviously doesn't agree.*

GAYLE. I'd rather not fly if it wasn't absolutely necessary.

MARKO. Oh, come on!

GAYLE. No! No 'come on'! You can't just swat it away like you do with everything. Or you can, but I can't. I wish I could. It's charming. But it's reckless. It's not me.

MARKO (*Pauses*). Wait . . . that's not . . . that's not why you moved? Closer to work? To avoid the tube?

GAYLE *is silent.*

MICHI (*to* TIASHA). I just want to understand you. I know about you, Tiasha.

TIASHA *looks at him, irritated.*

This city is big, yes, in geography. But really, people bring it down to size that fits them. And then it's no bigger than a village.

TIASHA. What do you want to know?

MICHI. Why you are doing this? Why you didn't go home?

TIASHA. Why don't you go home?

MICHI. It's different. I don't remember any more. It is years and years gone.

TIASHA. Exactly.

MICHI. Ahaha, no. That is not a fair answer.

TIASHA. Fair? You want a fair answer? You're a funny man, Michi. Besides, I thought in Michi's, discretion is important.

MICHI. All right. I respect your privacy. We say we are two orphans then. You and me.

TIASHA *nods. Pause.* MILA *gets up, walks to* MARKO, *embraces him.*

MILA (*to* MARKO). You stay, become a star.

MICHI (*thoughtfully*). I had big dreams for this place. I wanted Michi's to be the belly button of the wandering Eastern European soul.

MILA (*to* MARKO). And then come get me. Okay?

MICHI (*to* TIASHA). Instead, I am a whorehouse.

TIASHA. You make more money than ever, yes? Your clientele is British now, yes? What the hell you complain about. Business blossoms.

MARKO (*to* GAYLE). So, you're not going to go anywhere, you're not going to do art, you're not going to come with me, what are you going to do with yourself?

GAYLE. Help other people come here and stay. Noble, isn't it.

MICHI (*to* TIASHA). I don't like them beaten up.

TIASHA. They are not beaten up.

GAYLE (*to* MARKO). Actually, it is noble. Now, that I've started taking it seriously. It actually matters much more than . . . It matters.

MARKO *goes to leave.*

Marko . . . I don't . . . resent you. I just don't really understand you.

MARKO. So you turn your back.

GAYLE. Somebody died because we play stupid games. We always play stupid games.

MARKO. That's not why he died.

GAYLE. Well . . . as long as you're convinced . . .

MARKO. Bye, Gayle.

GAYLE. Bye, Marko.

GAYLE *fades out.*

MICHI (*to* TIASHA). Elena had bruises. I don't like it and it's very dangerous.

TIASHA. That was a mistake. Contact is changed. No one gets beaten up.

MICHI. You know what can happen to us if that gets out?

TIASHA. You just do your thing, you run the club, not much different from what you always do. Roman does his thing, he does network. I do mine. I do fieldwork. Everybody sticks to their bit, everybody is happy. All right?

MICHI (*resignedly*). Yes. Everybody happy. All right.

TIASHA. Trust me. It won't get out. It never gets out.

MILA *is on her way out carrying her luggage.* MARKO *walks over to her. They embrace.*

MILA. Come and get me and we'll start over. We'll be okay. Okay?

MARKO. Yes.

MILA *exits.* MARKO *fades out.*

ERIK. And, it's been three weeks. It's been sitting there for three weeks. It hasn't changed a bit. It's hot here, it's dusty and sticky and feels like you'd eventually rot away, danger, no danger. And every day, somebody doesn't come back. But the apple is still perfectly smooth and red. (*Beat.*) That's the only thing that hasn't happened before. Well, that and Baghdad. I've never been to Baghdad before.

ERIK *goes over to the wall in* GAYLE*'s office where* TIASHA*'s map still hangs. He shadows Iraq. He glances back at* MARTA. *She waves his packet of cigarettes at him. He goes back to her and sits down.*

Keep it. Really, keep it.

MARTA. Why? You want to quit?

ERIK *laughs.*

Bad for health?

MARTA *laughs loudly.* ERIK *joins her.*

ERIK. You know, it can kill you.

They both laugh harder.

I swear. It says so on the box. 'Smoking kills.'

Their laughter becomes hysterical.

MARTA. In every language in world. Everyone agree.

They slowly stop laughing. They wipe their tears away. They breathe deeply. ERIK *kisses* MARTA *on the forehead. He gets up and slowly walks out.* MARTA *produces an accordion and starts playing.*

Lights fade to black, the music plays on.

Epilogue

The South Bank.

MARTA *is sitting in the background, playing an accordion. She has a sign in front of her saying 'Pay as you listen'. The lights are bright, like on a sunny, early-autumn day.*

MARKO *and* MILA *are sitting on a bench drinking coffee from large paper cups.*

MILA. I like the Thames. It's powerful. You know, when I'm sitting here, with that view, with all those people, with those red buses running across the bridge, and with the music, I feel like I'm in a film. Like there's a camera following me, sipping my latte, deciding if I'm going to accept to play Cressida or . . . Cosette.

MARKO. Cosette?

MILA. Yes. I'll tell you about it on a rainy day.

MARKO. And it's sunny for days. What is that about fog in London? I don't see any fog.

MILA. The fog is a myth. But just wait for October to run out. Then the fun starts. Three, four straight months of rain, accompanied by large amounts of hail and the most annoying wind ever to blow on the Earth. It feels like a long long drizzly night.

MARKO. So, it's like Gotham City.

MILA (*laughs*). Yeah. Like Gotham City. You like the coffee?

MARKO. It's very . . . large and . . . milky.

MILA. They don't understand coffee. To them it's about froth and flakes and you know, things going on in a cup. They're not very . . . oral.

MARKO. What do you mean?

MILA. Well, you know they don't have a phrase for '*dobar tek*'.

MARKO. What do they say?

MILA. 'Bon appétit.' But they don't even say it that often because, you know, what's to look forward to?

MARKO (*laughs*). But it's good here?

MILA. It's good. Well, you have to be aware of this Mood . . . It's like this depressive mood that grabs you when things are not going too well. It makes you play native music and remember good things about home. It's very sneaky and you can never let your guard down.

MARKO. So, the Mood.

MILA. Yes. My boyfriend thinks it's the Slavic thing. He thinks we take things too seriously.

MARKO. I suppose he isn't Croatian.

MILA. Oh, no. I decided I will gravitate towards the west in every possible way.

MARKO. So what is your cure for the Mood?

MILA. You always believe in the plan.

MARKO. Which is?

MILA. I work out, I practise and I audition for musicals. Well, I audition, in general. Musicals would be a treat. Work hard, have faith and triumph – that's the plan.

MARKO. Aha. And this . . . Cassette is in the musical.

MILA. Cosette. Yeah. It was a dream. Ever since I was eight. Since I saw it in Zagreb. It was huge. And there were even children. You know – a boy and a girl. I pleaded with my mom to find out how it is you can get on a proper stage so young. My mom said – don't be silly, they're the director's

children, that's how. And, you know, for years I had this
fantasy that somehow I would find out that I was in fact a
director's child. But anyway, you probably think it's silly,
but I think there's something exhilarating about it and I
think that's . . . great.

MARKO. I don't think that's silly.

MILA. What's your dream?

MARKO *smiles, embarrassed.*

Go on.

MARKO. Well . . . I like . . . making people laugh. I think
making people laugh is one the rare things that make sense.
So, I guess a dream would be a stadium full of people who
laugh at me. I mean, with me. You know.

MILA (*smiles*). Those are big dreams, ha?

MARKO. Piece of pie.

MILA (*laughs*). It's 'piece of cake'.

MARKO (*smiles, embarrassed*). Oh.

MARKO *listens to* MARTA *playing the accordion.*

I like that woman.

*He gets up, goes over to her and puts some coins into her
box.*

MARTA. Thank you, son.

MARKO. You're welcome.

MARTA *plays on.*

You play beautifully. You make really good atmosphere.

MARTA. You are new in London, yes?

MARKO. How do you know?

MARTA. I know. People new in London, they feel awaken.
They feel – so much beauty, you have to share with
everyone. But in time, you will stop talking to beggars.

MARKO. You are not beggar.

MARTA. *Jesi ti, sine, naš?* [Son, are you one of us?]

MARKO. *Jesam. I vi ste!* [Yes. So are you!]

MARTA. *Našeg čovjeka odmah prepoznaš.* [You can always recognise one of our people.]

MARKO. *Neverovatno.* [What do you know.]

MARTA. *Lijepa ti je curica. Oću l' vam svirat neku našu?* [Pretty girl you got there. Shall I play one of our songs?]

MARKO (*cheerfully*). *Da. Da, da.* [Yes. Yes, yes.]

MARTA *starts playing.*

MARKO *goes back to* MILA.

MILA. That's . . . That's one of our songs.

MARKO. She's one of our people.

MILA. Is she?

MARKO. Yes. Amazing. Cigarette and it will be perfect. Want one?

MILA. I quit.

MARKO *lights a cigarette. They listen to the music and stare into the river.* MARKO *is visibly touched but happy.* MILA *is thoughtful.*

(*Snapping out of it.*) So, 'our people'. What do you mean by that?

MARKO. One of us.

MILA. We are going to get into a fight sooner or later, you do realise that?

MARKO. I'd love to get into a fight with you.

MILA. I'll win.

MARKO. Of course you will. You're a woman.

MILA. Exactly.

MARKO. I'll let you.

MILA. Oh God, we'll have to do some serious reprogramming. I fear my career will suffer.

They laugh.

MARKO. You'll be okay. I'm sure.

MILA. So will you. With your big dreams. You have any more as big?

MARKO. Just a couple. I think, if one comes true, the other can stay a fantasy. Be worth more in twenty years.

MILA (*smiles*). Twenty years is a long time. (*Pause.*) Have you got a place to live?

The end.

A Nick Hern Book

Fragile! first published in Great Britain in 2007 as a paperback original by Nick Hern Books Limited, The Glasshouse, 49a Goldhawk Road, London W12 8QP, in association with Cherub Company London

Reprinted 2016, 2023

Fragile! copyright © Tena Štivičić

Tena Štivičić has asserted her right to be identified as the author of this work

Cover photograph: © iStockphoto.com/cloki
Cover design: Ned Hoste, 2H

Typeset by Nick Hern Books, London
Printed in Great Britain by Mimeo Ltd, Huntingdon, Cambridgeshire PE29 6XX

A CIP catalogue record for this book is available from the British Library

The extract from Chekhov's *The Seagull* on page 51 is taken from Stephen Mulrine's translation, published by Nick Hern Books.

ISBN 978 1 85459 990 2